Pause and Reflect

Pause and Reflect

Your Guide to a Deeper Understanding of Early Intervention Practice

by

Dana C. Childress, Ph.D.
Partnership for People with Disabilities at Virginia Commonwealth University
Chesapeake, Virginia

·P A U L·H·
BROOKES
PUBLISHING C⁰ ®

Baltimore · London · Sydney

Paul H. Brookes Publishing Co.
Post Office Box 10624
Baltimore, Maryland 21285-0624
USA

www.brookespublishing.com

Typeset by Absolute Service Inc., Towson, Maryland.
Manufactured in the United States of America by
Versa Press, Inc., East Peoria, Illinois.

The individuals described in this book are composites or real people whose situations are masked and are based on the authors' experiences. In all instances, names and identifying details have been changed to protect confidentiality.

Library of Congress Cataloging-in-Publication Data

Names: Childress, Dana C., author. | Partnership for People with
    Disabilities, issuing body.
Title: Pause and reflect : your guide to a deeper understanding of early
    intervention practice / by Dana C. Childress ; Partnership for People
    with Disabilities at Virginia Commonwealth University, Chesapeake, Virginia.
Description: Baltimore : Paul H. Brookes Publishing Co., [2021] | Includes
    bibliographical references and index.
Identifiers: LCCN 2020058300 (print) | LCCN 2020058301 (ebook) | ISBN
    9781681254265 (paperback) | ISBN 9781681254272 (epub) | ISBN
    9781681254289 (pdf)
Subjects: LCSH: Children with disabilities—Services for—United States. |
    Caregivers—Services for—United States. | Parents of children with
    disabilities—Services for—United States. | Home-based family
    services—United States. | Children with
    disabilities—Development—United States. | Children with
    disabilities—Education (Early childhood)—United States.
Classification: LCC HV888.5 .C48 2021 (print) | LCC HV888.5 (ebook) | DDC
    362.3/30973—dc23
LC record available at https://lccn.loc.gov/2020058300
LC ebook record available at https://lccn.loc.gov/2020058301

British Library Cataloguing in Publication data are available from the British Library.

2025   2024

10   9   8   7   6   5   4   3

CONTENTS

About the Downloads

Purchasers of this book may download, print, and/or photocopy the Study Guide and Self-Assessments for educational use. These materials are available at http://downloads .brookespublishing.com for both print and e-book buyers.

1. Go to the Brookes Publishing Download Hub: http://downloads.brookespublishing.com

2. Register to create an account

   (Or log in with an existing account)

3. Filter or search for your book title

About the Author

Dana C. Childress, Ph.D., Early Intervention Professional Development Consultant, Chesapeake, Virginia

Dana Childress, Ph.D., is an early intervention professional development consultant with the Partnership for People with Disabilities at Virginia Commonwealth University. She has worked in the field of early intervention (EI) since 1995 as an educator, service coordinator, supervisor, trainer, author, and consultant. She is the coauthor of the book *Family-Centered Practices in Early Intervention: Supporting Infants and Toddlers in Natural Environments* (Paul H. Brookes Publishing Co., 2015), she writes the *Early Intervention Strategies for Success* blog, and she co-hosts the *EI on the Fly* podcast. Her interests include adult learning and EI service delivery, family-centered practices, supporting family implementation of intervention strategies, and finding ways to bridge the research-to-practice gap through interactive professional development for EI practitioners.

Preface

Ever had one of those visits when you got back in your car and just felt deflated? Frustrated? Or maybe puzzled about why the child is not making progress or the caregiver doesn't seem engaged? After sessions like that, it can be easy to explain away those feelings by placing the responsibility for what's happening on the family. Maybe the mother is on her phone more than she's talking with you. Maybe she says, "I don't know" when asked reflective questions. Maybe the child seems to prefer playing with you while the caregiver remains in the background. Caregivers absolutely have a primary role in early intervention (EI), but consider this: Caregivers generally do not know what they are supposed to do during visits. They often enter the system with no frame of reference for this kind of experience. A mother who stays out of the way may think this is "the expert's time" with her child. When she says, "I don't know," she might really mean it. When she is on her phone, she might be unsure of what else to do. When we see these things happening, the first thing to do is step back and reflect on what *you* are doing during the visit, because what you do and how you do it matter.

The service provider (e.g., educator, therapist, nurse) sets the tone and teaches the caregiver how EI works, and then the two of them collaborate to build the partnership. When it works well, it is a wonderful thing to see—a caregiver practicing using intervention strategies with her child during visits, with coaching and support from the service provider, and then successfully using those same strategies throughout the week. When it does not work so well, it can be frustrating for everyone. There are so many variables on any one visit that it's impossible to control them all. What we can control, however, is what *we* do during the visit. We are in charge of how we approach each session, where we focus our energy, and how we provide support. This book will focus on the *how* because how you collaborate with families affects what happens both during and between visits.

WHAT WE DO DURING VISITS AFFECTS WHAT THE CAREGIVER DOES BETWEEN VISITS

What we do during visits can significantly affect what caregivers learn and how they use intervention strategies with their children. When EI is conducted according to our field's mission and key principles (Workgroup on Principles and Practices in Natural Environments, 2008), we facilitate intervention that results in families who are confident and successful with engaging their children and using intervention strategies every day. That's not an easy task, especially when we are typically only with families for an hour or less a week, and the time we are trying to affect happens when we aren't even there. Achieving this kind of intervention requires that we consider all of the learners on a visit and how we can support their growth and development—and I'm not just talking about the children.

On every visit, you have at least two learners: the caregiver and the child (Childress, 2015). Chances are, you are already a rock star with facilitating infant and toddler learning. You've probably also thought about your role in helping caregivers use intervention strategies too, but have you really thought about how *caregivers* learn? For many of us, information about adult learning isn't something we get in our preservice education. To meet our mission, we need to intentionally engage caregivers in ways that also facilitate their learning so they know what to do with their children to encourage development every day. This requires more than having knowledge about infant and toddler development. For many of us, it requires that we add another set of skills to our toolbox, skills that come from a deep understanding of how caregivers learn. This book will focus on how you can facilitate caregiver learning so that families are ready to practice using intervention strategies during visits (with your support) and, more important, are able to use them when you aren't there. That's the key—making sure that the time we spend with families has the greatest impact on what they do with their children between visits. To do that, we have to focus on *both* learners.

MY STORY

Let me explain why I think this is so important. I've worked in EI for more than 25 years as an educator, service coordinator, supervisor, writer, and trainer. I spent the first 15 years of my career in direct service, working in three different EI programs in Virginia and in the first Educational and Developmental Intervention Services (EDIS) program at the Royal Air Force base in Alconbury, England. For the past 10 years, I've been an EI professional development consultant with the Partnership for People with Disabilities at Virginia Commonwealth University. I am part of our state's EI training team, so I develop resources and teach others how to "do" EI. I think *a lot* about what good EI looks like. I've written about it and taught about it, but nothing ever made me reflect on it more than when my son and I were receiving it. He had torticollis, so we received physical therapy until he was about 8 months old. I knew what I was supposed to do as a mom—use intervention strategies with my son—but I really struggled. I struggled to integrate the strategies our wonderful therapist taught me into our daily schedule. The whole day could go by and although I'd successfully kept my son alive, I'd completely forgotten to stretch him. Through that struggle, I learned about the importance of all of that time between visits and how necessary it is that we help families prepare to take advantage of those learning opportunities. This was also when I really understood the concept of the caregiver (i.e., other moms like me, dads, grandparents, child care teachers) as a learner too—because boy, did I have a lot to learn. The experience made me reflect on what I wanted to do differently with the families I supported at work. I wanted to make it easier for them between visits, so I had to change what I did during visits.

As time went by and our field evolved, I did my best to absorb all I could about routines-based early intervention (McWilliam, 2010) and coaching and consultation (Friedman, et al., 2012; Rush & Shelden, 2011), and think about how I could align my work with the mission of EI. Eventually, I transitioned to my current training and writing work, which pushed me to think more about the *why* of what we do. As a trainer, we think about how adults learn so that our trainings are effective. We know that adults always compare what they are learning to their prior knowledge and experience. We know that adults learn best when what they are learning is immediately useful and relevant. We also know that adults learn and retain information best through practice that includes reflection and feedback (Trivette et al., 2009). In thinking about all of this, a big lightbulb went on for me. The adult learning principles that I used to purposefully plan training activities could apply to EI visits as well. What if our service providers understood adult learning too? What if they applied adult learning principles and strategies to what they did during visits? As I studied adult learning and thought about how it applied to our work with families, it seemed to me to be a missing piece of the puzzle. It could help us be more effective in coaching families during visits so they are prepared for what to do between visits. I wondered, however, if we really understood more about how adults learned, would we be more effective coaches? I believe the answer is yes, and my dissertation research suggested the same.

WHAT'S COMING NEXT

As you move through this book, I invite you to take the time to pause and reflect on what you do, how you do it, and why. Reflection is an important part of professional growth and development, so on each visit ask yourself: *How am I helping this caregiver be successful using intervention strategies when I'm not here? How am I building his/her capacity? Am I supporting the caregiver's learning too?* Right now, you might not be sure of your answers, but don't worry; you have a journey ahead of you that will build your confidence. You are about to dive into adult learning theory and how it applies to your work. You'll learn about six adult learning principles and how to adapt your interactions with caregivers so they are learning right alongside their children.

In this book, I'll share practical strategies you can use during visits to prepare caregivers for intervening with their children between visits. You'll read real-world scenarios to help you compare what you are learning to what you do every day. You'll complete short self-assessments to challenge your beliefs about what you do and shine a light on what your actual practices look like. Because the hardest part of learning anything new is applying it, I'll guide you through lots of opportunities to pause and reflect on your current practice, think about new concepts, and plan for how to integrate what you are learning into what you do. The reflection activities throughout this book will give you space to dig deeper into your understanding of EI and really explore what it means to support caregivers and children. Finally, at the end of Chapters 1–5, you will find space to complete a reflection journal and a specific action plan to carry you forward.

It is my hope that as your knowledge of adult learning grows, your abilities to effectively facilitate learning for both caregivers and children will also blossom. I also hope that what you learn will help you do what you already do even better because remember, what you do and how you do it really do matter.

Acknowledgments

Writing this book has been a wonderful opportunity for my worlds to collide. I am so grateful to Paul H. Brookes Publishing for believing in my idea to combine my experience in early intervention (EI) with what I have learned from my professional development (PD) work and my doctoral research. I am especially grateful to my editor, Hudson Perigo, for her kindness, enthusiasm, and belief in my "voice." Hudson, you made this process delightfully easy. My appreciation extends to the other Brookes staff who worked with me throughout the process, from marketing to production to the folks who are always smiling at the conference vendor tables, making me feel giddy whenever I see my book on display.

I am also so very thankful for my colleagues on the Integrated Training Collaborative project at the Partnership for People with Disabilities at Virginia Commonwealth University. Cori, Deana, Lisa, Jeanne, Carrie, and Seb—I'm so proud of our team and feel lucky to call you colleagues and friends. Thanks especially to you, Cori, for believing in that exceptionally tall, gawky 21-year-old wearing the huge glasses who walked in for her very first "real job" interview at PACE so many years ago. You've been a special friend and colleague for so long. I appreciate you from the bottom of my heart.

So many faces and voices float through my head when I think about all of the other EI and PD colleagues I am so fortunate to know. Thank you for cheering me on, asking about my writing, and being smiling faces on the other end of endless Zoom meetings. To all of the families I have been so fortunate to partner with in the past—thank you for sharing your experiences with me. It was my honor and privilege to learn with you.

Finally, my heartfelt and deepest gratitude goes to my husband, Michael, and son, Caden, who were right there alongside me, always making space for me to write and pulling me away from the computer when I needed it. Michael, thank you for always being willing to come along with me, no matter what path I take. Thank you, too, for being my balance and my best friend, all while holding my heart. Caden, thanks for being the loudest voice cheering for me at graduation. I really love who you are, every funny, short (ha), and amazing part of you. You both mean the world to me.

With love and the deepest gratitude to my family for holding my hand, making me laugh, and frequently reminding me to pause

"

MANY ROADS LEAD
TO THE PATH, BUT
BASICALLY THERE ARE
ONLY TWO: REASON
AND PRACTICE.

"

—Bodhidharma

CHAPTER

1

Early Intervention as a Practice

*I*magine this scenario: You knock on the apartment door while listening to the scattering of feet inside and the cartoons being turned off. After a moment, the door opens and you are welcomed into the home. You sit beside the mother on the couch, greet the smiling toddler who leans against your knees, and start chatting about how their week has been. You ask about progress with the child's development and invite the mother to share updates on her efforts to use intervention strategies with her child that you practiced with her during the last visit. You ask what the mother would like to focus on today, and she says she would like help with ideas to encourage her son's communication while they play in the park across the street. It's a bright, sunny day, so the three of you head outdoors where you can observe this typical family routine. The visit is off to a great start.

Does this sound familiar? Do these types of interactions happen on most of your visits? Many of us who provide early intervention (EI) services have the privilege of supporting families with whom the interactions flow easily. When visits like this happen, you feel empowered as a professional and productive within the partnership you have established with the caregiver. There is nothing like working side by side with a caregiver who understands EI and embraces his or her roles as both an active learner and the person who is in the best position to make the biggest difference in the child's development. When the caregiver is ready and able to support the child's development through positive, responsive interactions provided in a stimulating environment, you have the perfect EI scenario.

Okay, now let's get real.

The truth is that not all intervention visits are so rosy. As you were reading the scenario, I wonder if you thought about visits where you've knocked, heard that familiar scattering of tiny feet, and kept knocking while no one came to answer the door. Or did you think about the times when a small child opened the door and told you that her mommy or daddy was sleeping? Did "turning the cartoons off" stick in your mind because of the visits during which you felt like you had to compete for attention with the television? Or perhaps you were reminded of the time when you entered the home, sat beside the mother, and then struggled for the next hour to connect and help her engage her child. On any given day, you can have visits that look like any of these examples, the rosy visit and the visits that are more challenging—and that's one of the things that makes this work so much fun. Every visit is different. Every family is different. Every interaction challenges you to use your knowledge and skills in a different way. Every visit is an opportunity to share your expertise, support caregiver–child interactions, and do something that could possibly have a lifelong impact for the child and family. You may not necessarily be the person who is in the best position to make the biggest difference, like the caregiver, but what you do and *how* you do it are important. The practices you use to engage families and the way you think about your work matters too.

EARLY INTERVENTION AS A PRACTICE

As service providers, we often think about our work in the context of a system of EI services and supports for infants and toddlers (ages birth to 36 months) with developmental delays or disabilities and their families. When people ask, "What do you do?" you may reply, "I work in early intervention"—which, of course you have to further explain because this field is such a specialty that most people have never heard of it.

Pause to PRACTICE

Instructions: Jot down a sentence or two that you use to describe your work to people you meet. Underline the key ideas, which you'll refer to later.

_____

_____

_____

_____

Is describing your work ❐ easy or ❐ difficult to do? Why?

As you read this book, I invite you to expand the way you think about your work to include the idea that EI is a *practice*. Think about how we refer to the practice of medicine, or how attorneys have a legal practice. These highly respected professionals are expected to stay current on research, precedent, and the growing evidence base for how to do their work most effectively. I would argue that early interventionists should be held to the same high standards. Regardless of whether you are a neurosurgeon or a speech-language pathologist, a lawyer or a special instructor, you have an ethical and professional responsibility to use your field's best practices. You must stay current, participate in professional development, and use what you learn through ongoing attention to the growing evidence base to support infants, toddlers, and families. What you learned in graduate school 5, 10, or 25 years ago was great back then but is not good enough now. You probably would not want to take your loved one to a doctor who graduated medical school 15 years ago and is still basing his recommendations on medical knowledge he learned back then. You expect your doctor to be constantly evolving his practice. The families you serve should expect no less.

Another way to think about EI as a practice is to compare it with the practices of meditation, mindfulness, and reflection. These practices focus on intentional, sustained efforts to be present and aware of your thoughts and actions. They also require you to think about what you do, how you do it, and why. Approaching professional development from these perspectives matches well with what Trivette et al. (2009) found in their research synthesis about the effectiveness of adult learning methods. They noted that *active participation* in what you are learning (intentional and sustained effort) and *reflection* on how what you learn compares to what you already do (self-awareness) are key ideas to help adult learners benefit from any kind of training opportunity. What I will be asking you to do in this book involves both intentional sustained effort and self-awareness. I won't necessarily ask you to meditate on what you learn (although there will be a guided meditation in Chapter 6), but throughout this book I will remind you to be mindful of how you think and to pay attention to what you do during visits. I will frequently ask you to be an active participant in your study of high-quality EI practices by providing opportunities to reflect on what you think and do and why you thought or did it. Let's briefly look at the practices of meditation, mindfulness, and reflection and think about how they connect to the work you will do here.

Meditation

Meditation has been referred to as the practice of training or calming the mind. According to Headspace.com (2019), meditation is "about training in awareness and getting a healthy sense of perspective." When you practice meditation, you take time to settle your mind and notice your thoughts without judging or changing them. You might sit still or take a walk while paying attention to your breathing and focusing your awareness on what you feel, hear, and see. As thoughts flow through your mind, you notice them and let them go without getting distracted by them. The purpose of meditation is to ultimately make you more aware of yourself and how you think while fostering a calm mind. It is a focused practice and one that takes time and effort to develop. Meditation is also something that only you can do for yourself. No one else can make you meditate or benefit from its practice. You choose that. Similarly, taking time to examine your thoughts and actions can be very valuable as you grow as a professional. Focusing on your practices as an early interventionist takes time and effort beyond the day-to-day work you do as you drive between visits, partner with families, monitor children's development, write contact notes, and so forth. Evolving your skills as an early interventionist requires a similar personal commitment. Think about it this way: Your supervisor can make you go to a workshop, but no one can make you use what you learn.

Mindfulness

Like meditation, practicing mindfulness is a choice a person makes to be aware of the present moment. Leaders in mindfulness, like Thich Nhat Hanh and Jon Kabat-Zinn, have described the practice as "dwelling in awareness" and "paying attention in a particular way: on purpose, in the present moment, and nonjudgmentally." Both leaders have also combined the concepts and described "mindfulness meditation." Situating EI as a practice in the contexts of mindfulness and meditation means that you build your awareness of what you think by purposefully attending those thoughts and what is happening inside of yourself. When you pay attention to your thoughts, feelings, and actions during interactions with families and other team members and while managing your workload, you can gain insights about yourself that you might have otherwise missed. Mindfulness and meditation encourage us to avoid judging our thoughts, feelings, and actions as they occur, but with increased awareness and some hearty reflection, you may come to realize what you are doing well, what is aligned with best practices, what you feel comfortable or uncomfortable with, and what you would like to do differently. Understanding these things about yourself can guide your professional development.

Reflection

Meditation and mindfulness can help you calm your mind and learn about yourself, but reflection is needed to help you dig deeper to investigate both how and why. It may not be enough to recognize that you feel frustrated or notice that you are thinking that working with a particular parent is really hard; if you want to do something with these thoughts and feelings to improve the situation, you have to take the time to reflect further to find out why you feel or think that way and how you got there. Reflection, especially with the help of a supportive supervisor or colleague, can help you gain valuable insights that often lead to problem solving and idea generation. Reflection can also help you recognize patterns with how you engage others, complete your work, or take care of yourself, patterns that may contribute to your success or interfere with it. Reflecting on the good things about our personal and professional lives can sometimes lead to identification of strategies we use in one situation that could be helpful in another.

The thing about reflection is this: It may or may not come naturally, but you can improve your ability to reflect through intentional practice. You will get the most out of your work here if you take the time to complete the reflection activities to guide your learning process. You may want to share your reflections with others, or you may not; individual reflection is valuable too. I will provide you with many opportunities to reflect on your thoughts, feelings, and actions related to working in EI. It will be up to you to decide what to do with what you learn.

I believe that adopting the idea of EI as a practice is essential to your ability to grow. It can empower you as a professional and motivate you to read that journal article, reflect on that last visit, reach out to others for support, and make your own professional development a priority. Because you have made the decision to read this book and work through this process, I'd say that you are already on the path to developing your practice. The first step is always the most important—good for you!

Pause
and REFLECT
Instructions: Before moving on to the next section, take a few moments to reflect on the idea that EI is a practice. Use these guiding questions to organize your thoughts or take your own path. Discuss this idea with a colleague for additional insights.

1. What are your thoughts about viewing early intervention as a "practice"? How might this perspective change the way you work with families? Prioritize professional development? Support new staff or students?

2. What would you like to be more mindful of in your EI practice? Why?

_____

_____

3. What would you like to learn more about? Why?

_____

_____

YOUR PRESERVICE PREPARATION
AND HOW IT AFFECTS YOUR PRACTICE

I mentioned that EI can be thought of as a system of services and supports. Before we begin to dig into your current practices, let's first think about your preservice preparation and how that affects your EI practice. EI operates according to guidance from the Individuals with Disabilities Education Improvement Act (IDEA) of 2004 (PL 108-446), which outlines requirements for the provision of federally funded services to infants and toddlers with developmental delays or disabilities and their families under Part C of the law. Because this is the same law that legislates special education services for older children, EI services were traditionally thought of as education or therapy for babies. There are a variety of service options available to eligible children and families, including special instruction (which is the educational service), physical therapy, occupational therapy, speech-language pathology, and so on, as well as service coordination (the only mandated service that all enrolled families receive). Over time, the work of EI service providers (such as special instructors and therapists) has evolved from child-centered sessions, during which the provider interacted primarily with the child while the caregivers passively observed, to more family-centered intervention. Now, we know from the work of experts in our field, such as Carl Dunst, Carol Trivette, Robin McWilliam, Dathan Rush, and M'Lisa Shelden, that EI is more likely to be successful when it is situated in the child's natural learning environment during daily activities and routines so that the caregiver can take the lead with the child while the EI practitioner provides coaching support. This is an important distinction that has come about as our work has evolved through research, experience, and listening to families about what works best for them. This evolution, however, means that how we provide support has had to change. You will learn more about this evolution in Chapter 2.

I often hear from practitioners that they were not trained well in family-centered intervention while in college or graduate school. Even though the concept of family-centered services has been around for a long time, helping students and new practitioners (and some of us more seasoned practitioners) understand how to implement it continues to be challenging. If you have been working in EI at all, you are probably aware that you are supposed to work with the caregiver and the child. In fact, our field's mission specifically tells us that "Part C early intervention builds upon and provides supports and resources to assist family members and caregivers to enhance children's learning and development through everyday learning opportunities" (Workgroup on Principles and Practices in Natural Environments, 2008). You probably know that family-centered intervention focuses on the link between a child's learning and the interactions and environments where most of that learning takes place. An infant's or toddler's family _is_ the context in which he or she learns. It is no longer considered best practice to go on an intervention visit, sit on the floor, and play with or exercise the child while talking to the parent for an hour. Don't get me wrong, this kind of intervention is not bad practice. I did EI for years that way because that was the best I knew how to do. This more traditional practice reflects how many of us were trained and honestly describes how many visits still are conducted today.

Pause and REFLECT

Instructions: Pause now to reflect on your two most recent intervention visits by answering the following questions:

1. What happened on my two most recent visits? What did the parent do? What did the child do? What did I do?

_____

_____

_____

_____

2. Where did I focus most of my energy—toward the child or parent or both? Why?

_____

_____

3. How does this match or not match with how I was trained to do my job during my university training?

_____

_____

Let's consider the preservice training of therapists. Physical therapists, occupational therapists, and speech-language pathologists receive training in how to work with patients across the life span. Those who focus on pediatrics still have a lot of years throughout the life span and developmental differences to learn about. Targeting preservice education to the EI population is almost impossible in these fields, so it is not uncommon for many therapy practitioners to receive little specific content or experience with how to provide EI services. It's not their fault, per se; it is just a matter of how university programs are structured and how much content can be taught in a limited amount of time. Preservice programs in these disciplines typically focus on how to work with the client—the child—while providing the caregivers (or other important adults like the child's teacher) with activities to do outside of the therapist's session (homework). This is similar to more traditional EI practice. With that said, many therapists have sought out additional training after entering the field to build their knowledge and skills related to family-centered practices and use this information to provide high-quality EI services. Where you start does not necessarily define where you end up, but those beginnings lay the foundation for your professional practice so deserve some acknowledgment and reflection.

For the professionals who provide special instruction, the challenges are both similar and quite different. If your background is in early childhood special education (like mine), you may have learned about multiple aspects of this particular field—EI and preschool special education—for children ages birth to 5 years old. Some of you may have also learned about teaching children up to age 8. Like our therapist colleagues, there is a lot to learn about children in these age ranges. Some programs focus content, practica, and student teaching experiences more heavily on the preschool (and early elementary school) age ranges, whereas others try to balance what students learn to include strategies for supporting development across the age range. These programs typically focus on how to work with the student—the infant or toddler in EI—and how to assess development, how to write goals on the child's service plan, what teaching strategies to use to encourage the child's development, and so forth. More and more programs are integrating family-centered practices and conveying the mission and key principles of EI, which are essential for educators (and all practitioners) to understand. When this happens, students are more likely to be better prepared to use the field's best practices and that is important.

Here's the rub and where we differ from the therapy disciplines.

Across the United States, there are no consistent educational, professional knowledge or experience requirements for those who provide special instruction. States define these requirements, which results in practitioners providing this service with a wide range of preparation and skills (or sometimes, lack thereof). State requirements range from a high school diploma to a graduate degree. Some states required related knowledge and skills when hiring, whereas others only require a certain degree level (meaning that you can provide special instruction with a business degree, for example). As you can imagine, this leads to vastly different practices being used (and not used) with children and families. As I noted with therapists, there are many skilled special instructors who entered the field fully prepared or who make a conscious decision to seek out in-service training to build their knowledge and skills after they begin working with children and families—and many others who do both.

Pause
to PRACTICE

Instructions: Think back to your university training. Without judging it as good or bad, add a mark on the line to indicate how much of your training focused on EI, and then complete the statements.

None ◄--► All

During my university training, the information I learned about early intervention focused on

_____

_____

Before starting this work, I wish I had known more about

_____

_____

Whether you are one of the practitioners with the high school diploma or graduate degree on your wall, or you came to the field with little or lots of experience, there is always room for you to evolve your practices. If you entered the field without preservice training, you will have to build your knowledge and skill base. If you entered the field with strong pre-service training as a therapist or educator, you will still have to build your knowledge and skills. Why? Because this field is always changing and growing. We are still learning about our field's evidence-based practices. Even if you think you know tons about EI, how you use what you know is different from visit to visit. You bring your professional practices, knowledge, and skills to each visit and adapt them to what the family brings, which are their unique ways of interacting, their priorities for their child and themselves, and their hopes for the future. One of the biggest challenges with working in EI is figuring out how to take what you know and what you know how to do—your expertise—and share it with families in a way that they can understand and use every day. Your ability to face that challenge visit after visit may have been grounded in your preservice training, but how you overcome that healthy challenge and even revel in it may be linked with your beliefs about your role, your awareness of and reflections on your practices, and what you choose to do with this information when you provide EI services. Next, let's dig a little deeper and think about your role as an EI practitioner.

YOUR ROLE AS AN EARLY INTERVENTION PRACTITIONER

Your beliefs about your role as an EI practitioner or provider (I will use both labels in this book) set the tone for everything you do with families. Think back to what you wrote earlier in this chapter about how you describe your job to others. What key ideas did you underline? Add your key ideas to the Pause to Practice table that follows, and then draw a line to match them to similar ideas on either side. This will help you identify whether your beliefs about your role fall into a more traditional, child-focused way of thinking or a more family-centered way of thinking.

Pause
to PRACTICE

Family-Centered Practices	Your Key Ideas	Child-Focused Practices
I work with the caregiver and child during visits.		I play with babies.
I support child development through caregiver–child interactions as much as possible.		I work with children to help them learn to walk, talk, eat, play, etc., while the caregiver mostly watches.

I use coaching strategies to help caregivers practice using intervention strategies with the child during visits so they know what to do between visits.		I bring toys and books to visits to ensure that the child and I have appropriate materials for learning (and then take them with me so I can clean them after the visit).
I join family routines and activities, and I use what the family has in the home to promote learning.		I work with the child mostly through toy play in the living room.
I provide information so the caregiver can make informed decisions.		I provide caregivers with homework they can do between visits.

Without judgment, what did you notice about your beliefs? Did your key ideas tend to be linked more with one side of the table or the other? Or perhaps you noticed a mixture of beliefs. Now, compare your beliefs to what you described earlier when you reflected on two of your most recent visits with families. Perhaps you noticed that your beliefs and your actions line up well. Or maybe you see a conflict between your beliefs and your actions— for instance, you know that current thinking about EI practice suggests that we join family routines during visits, but most of your visits tend to "look like" toy play on the living room floor. Implementing what we believe is not always easy and is affected by many variables, such as the resources and learning opportunities available in the environment, our com- fort level with doing something other than toy play, the caregiver's own beliefs and pref- erences about what is supposed to happen on a visit, and even the outcomes that we are addressing on the individualized family service plan (IFSP). What is important here is to be aware of what you bring to the parent–service provider relationship because you will set the tone for the interactions that happen on your visits.

If you believe that you are the expert and it is your role to work with the child to address the IFSP outcomes, then your visits are more likely to be child focused. Yes, you did go to school for many years to gain your expertise and no, you can't teach a parent all that you learned (I've heard this argument more than once). However, if only you provide the child with intervention, then the child is only receiving supportive learning opportunities once or twice a week (or even less depending on when you visit), which translates to not very often. Service providers using this model may explain to parents what they are doing with the child during visits (aka "modeling") and hope that the parent sees and understands enough to be able to use the same strategy with the child between visits. Dathan Rush from the Family Infant and Preschool Program has called this "hopeful modeling"—we model with the hope that the parent can figure out how to do what we do. Here's the prob- lem with this approach: It does not align well with what we know about how adults learn.

Most of the caregivers you work with will be adults, and despite our tendency to seek out YouTube whenever we have a problem to solve, adults just do not learn best through passive observation. According to adult learning theory as described by Knowles, Holton, and Swanson (2012), we are active, self-directed learners, meaning that we prefer to drive our own learning experiences and be active participants, getting our "hands dirty" to try out what we are learning and make it our own. Watching another person has its benefits, but being able to try out what we observe is more likely to help adult learners integrate what they are learning into what they do every day. This matters with regard to how you approach your work with families.

If you believe that your role is to share your expertise by working more directly with both the caregiver and the child in the context of their interactions, then your visits are more likely to be aligned with family-centered practices. When you partner with the caregiver to facilitate the child's learning during interactions that are similar to what happens between visits, you are more likely to expand the intervention the child receives beyond the visit. We want each child to have as many opportunities to learn and practice skills, interact with others, and use his or her abilities in as many different contexts as often as possible. You can lay the groundwork for this by supporting learning for both the caregiver and the child, joining activities that they enjoy and activities that they find challenging, problem solving together, sharing what you know about child development and intervention, and coaching the caregiver as he or she practices using strategies with the child. This is an important distinction that we will explore in Chapter 3.

YOUR PURPOSE AS EARLY INTERVENTION PRACTITIONERS

Pause
and REFLECT   *Instructions*: How would you describe your purpose as an EI practitioner? Use this space to list words and phrases that are meaningful to you, or illustrate your purpose with a drawing.

I believe that our purpose as EI practitioners is to share what we know about child development and intervention in a way that builds the capacity of the caregiver to support the child's learning every day, including (most importantly) when we are not there. Sure, we could probably teach the child to walk, talk, eat, and play on our own, but we know that the child learning to do something only when the service provider is there really doesn't matter. What matters is whether children can use their skills and abilities to do things that are important to their families, like walk to the car before going on family errands, talk about what they want and need, eat dinner with their family each evening, and play and learn with their favorite toys and people. If we can build on what caregivers and children already do, help caregivers learn to think about how they engage their children and understand the impact their interactions have, and teach and practice strategies that the caregiver can use with the child, then we will be providing family-centered services that reach far beyond any single visit.

With that said, I don't think this is easy. To do the real work of EI in a way that meets our field's mission, we have to become more aware of what *we* are doing and hold this purpose in mind before we knock on each family's door. We must commit to being professional learners who are mindful of the practices we use with families and the perspectives we bring into the home. We must continually reflect on that work and our role in supporting learning for all of the learners on a visit. It's easy to take for granted that the way we choose to interact with families matches with our field's recommended practices. We all think we do great work, and we probably do. If you really want to know that you do great work, then make time for reflection to build your awareness of what you do, how you do it, and the impact your work has on others. I hope that as you move through this reflective guide, you will learn about yourself as a professional while also learning about high-quality EI service delivery. I encourage you to keep this book handy so you can use it as a reflective journal to capture your thoughts before and after visits. Take a few minutes each day to read and work through the activities. As you gain a deeper understanding of the important work you do, you will also be growing your EI practice. You've taken your first step here. Now, let's jump in.

YOU DON'T NEED ENDLESS TIME AND PERFECT CONDITIONS. DO IT NOW. DO IT TODAY. DO IT FOR TWENTY MINUTES AND WATCH YOUR HEART START BEATING.

—Barbara Sher

Reflective Journal

Instructions: Use this space to capture your thoughts about what you learned in Chapter 1.

NEW IDEAS: _____

_____

_____

_____

_____

_____

IDEAS THAT CHALLENGED ME: _____

_____

_____

_____

_____

_____

THOUGHTS & FEELINGS: _____

_____

_____

_____

_____

_____

Action Plan

Instructions: Based on your reflections in this chapter, what do you want to do next? Make a commitment to yourself with this first action plan. When you complete your action plan, come back and celebrate it here.

By _____ (date),

I will take responsibility for growing my early intervention practice by learning more about _____

_____(knowledge or practice)

by _____ (action).

(action examples: reading an article, watching a webinar, shadowing a colleague, etc.)

ACTION PLAN COMPLETED ☐

My key takeaway: _____

_____

_____

TIPS:

- Set a weekly reminder in your phone or on your calendar to check in with yourself on your progress.
- Ask a colleague to learn with you to keep you accountable.
- Once you have met your goal, share what you learned with a colleague and discuss how to use the information in practice with families and other team members.

"

SUCCESS IS NEITHER MAGICAL NOR MYSTERIOUS. SUCCESS IS THE NATURAL CONSEQUENCE OF CONSISTENTLY APPLYING THE BASIC FUNDAMENTALS.

"

—Jim Rohn

Fundamentals of Early Intervention Practice

You may be tempted to skip this chapter. As an experienced EI practitioner, I know I would be. You may already feel like you have a firm grounding in fundamentals like family-centered practices, intervention strategies, and how to use your knowledge and skills in natural environments, especially if you have been practicing EI for a while. Before you turn to Chapter 3, pause and ask yourself: *How often do I have (or take) the opportunity to reflect on what I know and how well I am using it?* If you sighed and thought, "Well, not very often because I have to (insert all the things that keep you busy)," then you are likely not alone. The truth is that most EI practitioners are hopping from one intervention visit to the next, conducting assessments and IFSP meetings, and squeezing documentation in during valuable office time, while sitting in their cars between visits, or in the evenings "after" work. Reflection on practice might not be a high priority with other important demands on your time—demands that themselves are time bound, such as entering contact notes in the record within a certain number of days or making sure services start in a timely manner. This chapter will provide you with an equally important opportunity to dive deeper into fundamental concepts that guide the provision of high-quality EI services. More importantly, it will offer you the space to think about how you—as an individual service provider—implement these concepts and what they look like when you implement them day to day. Give yourself this time because what you do in the subsequent chapters will build on the mental work you do here.

Let's start by warming up your brain.

Instructions: Circle or highlight the 20 words in the word cloud (Figure 2.1) that match fundamental concepts for EI. To check your answers, visit page 157.

FIGURE 2.1. Fundamentals word cloud.

Pause
and REFLECT   *Instructions:* Based on the words you circled, choose 3–5 words that you think are important to high-quality, effective EI practices. List them below and describe why they are important. Then, revisit the word cloud and choose 3–5 words that challenge you or words that you need to know more about. These may or may not be words you circled. List those words and note why you chose them (i.e., what you want to learn, why they challenge you). It is okay if you have the same words on both lists.

Important words	Challenge words
Why are these important?	**Why are these challenging?**
Notes:	Notes:

As you read this chapter (and the rest of the book), keep an eye out for the words on both of your word lists. Open yourself up to learning more about these words. Underline or highlight them when they pop up, and come back to this page to add notes about the words you chose as you gain a deeper understanding of how they fit into fundamental EI practices.

THE MISSION OF EARLY INTERVENTION

When you think about the work you do, how would you describe the mission of EI? Think bigger than just what you do. Think about how you would capture the goal of the work. Complete the statement below with your description of the mission. On the surface, this might seem similar to how you described what you do in Chapter 1, but I encourage you to back up your lens and think about the field as a whole.

Pause
and REFLECT   The goal (or mission) of EI is: _____

_____

_____

Now, let's compare what you wrote with the mission of EI that was developed in 2008 by a group of EI leaders:

> *Part C early intervention builds upon and provides supports and resources*
> *to assist family members and caregivers to enhance children's learning*
> *and development through everyday learning opportunities.*
> *(Workgroup on Principles and Practices in Natural Environments, 2008, p. 2)*

Even though the year of publication may lead you to think it is outdated, this seminal mission has been widely adopted across our field as a statement that grounds what we do and hints at why we do it. It is essential that practitioners really grasp the message in the mission because it can change your perspective on what you do and *how* you do it. Take about 10 seconds and underline or highlight (I love highlighters) the key words you notice in the mission. How do the words you just highlighted compare with your important words and your challenge words from the word cloud?

   According to this mission statement, what we do is "assist family members and caregivers to enhance children's learning and development." This part of the statement is critical because it emphasizes that our work focuses on engaging with families and other caregivers, not playing with, stretching, or prompting babies. As I mentioned in Chapter 1, many EI practitioners were trained to focus on the child as the student or client, but according to this mission, your focus should also be on the parent, child care provider, grandparent, and so forth. The caregiver is the person who has the most opportunities to make the biggest difference in the development of the child because he or she interacts with the child much more frequently than you do. The caregiver and child have hours together every day, whereas you may have 45–60 minutes together a week (or less). Yes, amazing things can happen in that one hour, but if that is where all of your energy is focused, and that is when the family believes the difference in the child's development happens, then you (and they) could be missing out on many opportunities during which the child could be learning and intervention could be happening.

The caregiver is the person who has the most opportunities to make the biggest difference in the development of the child.

Pause
and REFLECT *Instructions:* Think about a typical intervention visit. Mark the lines below to get a sense of where you focus during the visit. Note what percentage of time you think you spend engaging the caregiver and the child. Be honest with yourself and consider why you choose to focus your time in this way, without judging your focus or judging the caregiver's contribution. This is about you, not the caregiver.

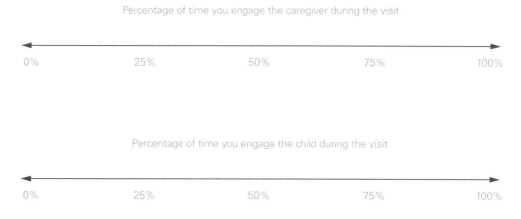

Percentage of time you engage the caregiver during the visit

| 0% | 25% | 50% | 75% | 100% |

Percentage of time you engage the child during the visit

| 0% | 25% | 50% | 75% | 100% |

Now, using the box below, jot down the reasons why you think you marked the lines the way you did. Try to focus on your own beliefs, thoughts, and behaviors when you write your "whys" rather than focusing on what the caregiver does or does not do. For example, rather than writing, "The mother is always texting on her phone," which, while it may be true, places blame squarely on the caregiver and absolves you from any responsibility in the situation. Instead, consider your own actions and challenges, such as "I have a hard time finding ways to keep the mother engaged," which can help you reflect on how you feel and point you in the direction of what you might be able to do differently to work toward better engagement with the parent and the child.

Reasons why:

One thing you want to do differently:

Years ago, as I was trying to break away from my toy bag and make sure that my practices were better aligned with recommended practices, I came across an article written by Robin McWilliam (2000). In the article, he emphasized a point that I think I knew deep inside but had not really fully understood. He said that it is not what the service provider does in the home that will make the difference in the child's development; it is what the family, child care providers, and others learn during the sessions and use during their activities and routines throughout the week that facilitates the child's learning and development. Along with the mission, this fundamental truth reminds us that our work should be balanced between supporting the child's learning and development (so yes, we will play, stretch, and prompt the baby) while facilitating interactions between the caregiver and the child (so that the caregiver understands how to play, stretch, and prompt said baby). Those interactions are the vehicle for the child's development. Most EI practitioners recognize this—the challenge can be in finding ways to affect those interactions during visits so that the caregiver knows what to do with the child and how to do it during the "everyday learning opportunities" (mentioned in the mission statement) that happen between visits when the service provider is not there.

> Interactions between the caregiver and the child are
> the vehicle for the child's development.

Pause to LEARN

Instructions: This might be a good place to pause and take time to learn more about the mission of EI and the key principles that guide its implementation. If you are not already familiar, review the following documents, which you can easily find online by searching for their titles:

- Agreed Upon Mission and Key Principles for Providing Early Intervention Services in Natural Environments

- Seven Key Principles: Looks Like/Doesn't Look Like

- Agreed Upon Practices for Providing Early Intervention Services in Natural Environments

Or, if you prefer to complete a short online module, look for the "Overview: Mission and Key Principles" module on the Virginia Early Intervention eLearning Center site (https://veipd.org/elearn/). Create an account and then access the free module to learn more. When you are ready, come back here to capture your thoughts.

1. Which key principle(s) most intrigued you? Why?

    _____

2. Which key principle(s) "look like" how you practice?

    _____

3. Which key principle(s) "doesn't look like" how you practice?

    _____

4. What are two things you will do on your next visit to ensure that you are implementing the mission and key principles?

    1. _____

    2. _____

FUNDAMENTALS OF EARLY INTERVENTION PRACTICE

Family-Centered Practice and Individualized Intervention

One of the things I like about the mission statement of EI is that, in a single sentence, it captures fundamental concepts that guide our practices. The mission's emphasis on assisting family members and other caregivers points to a family-centered, capacity-building approach. This approach emphasizes the substantial effect that family interactions, activities, and environments have on a child's development (Bailey et al., 2012; Bronfenbrenner, 1986; Bruder, 2010; Moore et al., 2014; Odom & Wolery, 2003; Yang et al., 2013). The use of family-centered, capacity-building practices has been associated with positive outcomes for children and families (Dunst et al., 2014; Swanson et al., 2011), and these practices have been a central component of high-quality intervention for many years.

> We combine what we know about child development and intervention
> with what the caregiver knows about the child and family.

When we use family-centered practices, we embrace the ideas that families are the most important "agents of change" for the child's development and that their decisions, preferences, interests, and interactions guide our work. When we operate from a capacity-building perspective, we interact with caregivers in ways that are responsive to what is important to them and what they want their child to be able to do (Dunst et al., 2014). We respect families' cultural values and beliefs and acknowledge the important role they play in how caregivers parent their children. We combine what we know about child development and intervention with what the caregiver knows about the child and family. The result of this collaboration means that we are building the capacity of the caregiver to interact with his or her child in ways that positively impact development every day, during the daily routines and activities that happen as part of natural family life. When we provide EI services, we partner with caregivers during intervention visits to practice and refine intervention strategies, so caregivers are well prepared to support their child's development during and between visits, when most children's learning occurs (McWilliam, 2010). Without family-centered, capacity-building practices, we are just "doing therapy" to kids and hoping it sticks. With these practices, we have opportunities to make a much more significant impact on the child's development by working with and through the caregiver. How do we do this? By building on what families already do.

> The onus is on us to find the strengths that each family has, recognize them for the resources they are, and then adapt our knowledge of intervention to build on those strengths.

The mission statement starts by reminding us to "build upon" what the family does to encourage the child's development. It's true that some families enter EI with interactions in place that are easier to build upon and that other families need more resources and support. The onus is on us, however, to find the strengths that each family has, recognize them for the resources they are, and then adapt our knowledge of intervention to build on those strengths. When we mindfully enter a relationship with a family from the perspective that we are there to discover and build on what they already have in place (their interactions, materials, routines, and activities), then that alters the work we will do. It heightens the importance of the caregiver–child relationship and the individualized nature of the work.

What Does Implementation Look Like?

Let's consider two intervention visit scenarios with the same practitioner and family. As you read, notice how the service provider implements (or does not implement) the mission of EI, family-centered, capacity-building practices, and individualized intervention. Each scenario will be followed by questions to help you gather your thoughts and compare what you read with what you have learned so far.

Pause
to PRACTICE   Eli is visiting with Selina and her 18-month-old son, Max. During the visit, Selina mentions that she has been struggling to get Max to sit in his car seat. She said Max tends to arch his back and tantrum, which makes it very hard to buckle him in. Because Max is not yet using many words to communicate, Selina is not sure what is wrong and feels frustrated that they cannot easily get in the car to run errands. Eli asks if Selina would like some help with this and Selina emphatically says, "Yes!"

Scenario 1: Eli asks Selina if she has tried to give Eli toys or books to distract him while she puts him in the car seat. She says she has tried that and he throws them. Eli suggests that Selina have a snack ready so she can give it to Max as soon as he is sitting in the car seat to keep him busy while she buckles him in. Selina says she will try that but she thinks that he will probably just throw that too. Eli tells Selina that is it typical for 18-month-old children to try to exert some independence and that if she is firm and loving, this will pass and Max will settle down eventually. Eli then shifts the conversation back to Max's communication and resumes playing with Max in the living room floor while Selina sits nearby.

1. Was Eli successful with implementing the mission of EI? Why or why not?

---

2. What could Eli have done differently to embed family-centered, capacity-building practices into the visit?

Turn to page 161 to compare your answer with mine.

Now, let's consider what might have happened if Eli had taken a different approach.

Scenario 2: Eli asks Selina what she has already tried to manage this challenge. Selina says she has tried giving Max a toy he likes or her phone to play with, but he will throw them once she puts him in the seat. She has tried telling Max to stop fussing but that just seems to make them both more upset. Eli asks if he can watch their typical routine for getting in the car. Selina tells Max that they are going for a ride and they begin to get ready. Selina puts on Max's shoes, grabs the diaper backpack, then picks up Max and carries him to the car. She opens the minivan door, puts the backpack inside, and then tries to put Max in his car seat. Before his bottom gets to the seat, he begins to thrash and fuss. Selina's voice raises so she can be heard over his fussing and she tells him to calm down. She tries to keep Max in his seat but he arches and slides out. They continue to tussle until Selina turns to Eli and says, "See what I mean?"

In both scenarios so far, Eli has not really been much help. In Scenario 1, he throws a few strategies at the wall but none really stick. These are probably suggestions Eli would offer any family. In Scenario 2, he has acknowledged the mother's prior efforts and observed the challenge, but if he stops here, nothing has really changed. Eli must take the conversation further, avoiding the instinct to start making suggestions right away while he learns more about what is going on. Let's see how Scenario 2 continues with a conversation designed to dig deeper so Eli can individualize intervention and ultimately build the mother's capacity to find a solution to improve the routine.

While Max plays in the backyard, Eli and Selina talk about what just happened. Eli asks Selina about how Max gets into other seats, such as his high chair or up onto the couch. She said that he recently started climbing into his high chair and trying to buckle himself in. Eli and Selina talk about how 18-month-olds often want some control and how it is very typical for them to try to exert some independence. The trick is to find ways to help them feel independent while still getting done what needs to be done. Because Max is still learning to use early words to communicate, he can get frustrated very easily, so Eli and Selina try to think of ways they can help Max take the lead and communicate what he wants when getting ready for a ride. Eli notes how Selina has done that with the high chair by letting Max seat himself. Selina decides to try to let Max climb into the car and into the seat himself while she prompts him for simple words that match what he is doing.

Selina picks up Max and starts to bring him to the car. Eli suggests that she let Max walk while she holds his hand, which also gives Max some control. Selina tries this and talks to Max as they get closer to the door. She uses a gentle voice to ask Max if he wants to climb up into the van like a big boy. She opens the door and Max tries to climb in. Eli coaches Selina to provide as little help as possible. For example, Selina places her hand under Max's foot to help him climb from the driveway into the car. Selina says "up?" and "seat" while pointing to the car seat to encourage Max. He scrambles into the seat and then Selina and Eli cheer, which causes Max to clap. Eli suggests that Selina let Max sit in the seat for a few minutes so he can get used to being there without feeling stressed. Selina gives Max his cup of goldfish from the backpack. After he finishes his snack, she asks Max if he can help her with the buckles. He finds the buckles and lets Selina put his arms through them. When Selina is not sure how to let Max help, Eli models how to use hand-over-hand support to help Max click the buckles together. They cheer again, then unbuckle Max and let him climb out by himself. Eli gives Max a high-five and asks Selina how she thinks that went. She smiles and says that she likes letting Max climb in. Eli tells Selina that she did a great job with letting Max feel like a big boy and with modeling simple words for him. This involves Max in the process so he does not feel like the process is being done to him. Selina and Eli talk about plans for when Selina can practice this new routine before trying to go for a real ride. Selina plans to practice it 1–2 times a day and let Eli know how it goes next week.

1. Was Eli successful with implementing the mission of EI? Why or why not?

    _____

    _____

2. Which family-centered practices did Eli use to build Selina's capacity to solve the problem?

    _____

    _____

3. What percentage of time did Eli spend engaging the caregiver? The child?

    a. _____

    b. _____

4. What are the main differences between Scenarios 1 and 2? Why do these differences matter?

    _____

    _____

    _____

5. Which scenario best matches how you conducted your last three visits? Be honest. _____

6. What do you want to keep reflecting on? _____

    _____

Turn to page 162 to compare your answers to Questions 1–4 to mine.

In these scenarios, we see two very different outcomes. In Scenario 1, Selina expresses her concern but receives limited support because the session is more child focused.

In Scenario 2, Eli embraces the mission of EI and recognizes the learning opportunity inherent in the car seat routine. He focuses on both learners during the visit and situates intervention in the context of the parent–child interaction. He observes the troublesome routine and then has a reflective conversation to learn more. He uses what he learns to coach Selina through using several interventions strategies, which not only gets closer to a solution to her problem but also opens up a new learning opportunity for Max. Perhaps most important, if this process results in an easier routine for the family, quality of life will improve because they regain their ability to easily leave the home to run errands. The difference between the scenarios is powerful and all goes back to a family-centered, capacity-building approach.

Everyday Learning Opportunities and Routines-Based Intervention

The mission of EI also points out that a child's development is situated in the everyday learning opportunities that naturally occur through interactions with the environment and people around him or her. You have just read a great example of this with Max's story. The activities that happen every day are the ones during which children learn the skills they need to participate in the family life. Even though we cannot join every activity or see every routine, we can approach intervention with openness and curiosity to look for those natural learning opportunities and help families learn to seize them. This can be easy with families who have many rich routines and activities; it gets harder when we support families with less variety to their routines or who give us access to only one or two routines (playtime and television watching, for instance). This can also be challenging when cultural differences or family preferences related to routines and activities feel different from our own way of doing things.

> Even though we cannot join every activity or see every routine, we can approach intervention with openness and curiosity to look for those natural learning opportunities and help families learn to seize them.

In the more challenging situations, we can be very tempted to bring a book or a bottle of bubbles to the home so that we have something "instructional" to do to stimulate the child. I'll be honest, I can teach almost any child to engage with me with bubbles and a wand, but what does that matter if the child cannot engage with his or her family when I am not there? It doesn't. What does it matter if the child and family never ever play with bubbles except during the visit? Well, it probably matters very little unless the bubble activity is a teaching tool that is followed by planning and practice to help the caregiver generalize what was learned. In Max's scenario, if Eli had been successful getting Max into his car seat but Selina was not able to do it, then Eli's accomplishment really would not be all that helpful or impactful. Same with me just blowing bubbles for fun with the child. However, engaging over a fun game of bubbles that includes the caregiver and the child can be an effective intervention technique *if* the caregiver is actively participating and is learning strategies such as how to use wait time effectively, how to prompt the child for an initial sound, or how to motivate a child to squat to reach that big bubble. If I am the only one using these techniques, then the child is only learning from me. We know that infants and toddlers learn best when they have repeated opportunities to learn and practice new skills. If the caregiver learns the strategies then generalizes them to other daily routines, with our support and with intentional planning and practice, then we are building the capacity of that caregiver to spread intervention well beyond our single visit. It's not about bubbles or car seats; it's about looking for opportunities for learning for both the caregiver and the child that can be replicated and practiced during and between visits.

Now let's go a little deeper. Any discussion of "everyday learning opportunities" must also include a look at routines-based EI (McWilliam, 2010). With one raised eyebrow, a purist might question my mention of using bubbles on a visit, asking if I brought the bubble bottle to the visit or used bubbles the family already owned. Did I use a play or engagement routine that was already in place or did I try to create a new one? Routines-based intervention encourages practitioners to learn about the daily routines and activities of each family then use that information to look for opportunities during which the child's development can be encouraged while addressing goals that have been identified by the family. This type of intervention is grounded in another key concept, natural learning environment practices (NLEPs). According to Carl Dunst and his colleagues (2001), NLEPs focus on taking advantage of the natural interactions that occur between caregivers and children during daily activities. Routines-based intervention takes this a step further to look at specifically what is happening during those interactions in the child's natural environment. It is in the context of those everyday interactions and routines that children learn and grow. If we, as EI practitioners, can tap into these natural interactions and routines, we are more likely to have a bigger impact on the child's development than we could if we only focused on the interactions and contrived routines that occur during our visits. There is an emphasis on contextualizing intervention—meaning that we make sure that intervention happens in the context of what is meaningful and natural for the family. When we assist caregivers by building on natural learning opportunities and supporting their daily interactions with their child, we are working toward the mission of EI. How we do this is the big question.

> If we can tap into natural interactions and routines, we are more likely to have a bigger impact on the child's development than if we only focus on the interactions and contrived routines that occur during our visits.

Let's go back to the bubbles. If the family had the bubbles and already enjoyed playing with them with the child before the visit, then score one for routines-based intervention. I would have been taking advantage of an existing play routine and helping the caregiver practice integrating intervention strategies to boost learning during an activity the caregiver and child already enjoy. This can be very effective because in this scenario, the caregiver does not have to learn a new activity plus learn new intervention strategies, thus decreasing the cognitive load of having to learn two new things at once. She and her child already know what to do to enjoy blowing bubbles together, maybe out in the backyard, during bath time, or just when hanging out in the living room after naptime. I can build on that knowledge and experience by modeling and coaching the caregiver on how to, for example, gently withhold blowing the bubbles while prompting the toddler to try to say the /b/ sound for bubble, use a sign, or look in her direction to get her to blow more. Practicing these new strategies with my support can offer an important learning opportunity for both the caregiver and child, which can be followed by a discussion about how and when she could use the withholding strategy during other routines (e.g., before giving more goldfish for snack, refilling the sippy cup of water, or picking the child up to put him in the high chair). When you take advantage of an existing activity like this, you make it easier for the caregiver and child to learn and practice the new skills and use them later because you have built on something familiar.

Now, let's consider the value of introducing bubbles as a new play activity that the caregiver had not tried before. On one hand, introducing something new might be fun, but it might also be less likely for the caregiver to do it between visits because it is new. It might be harder for her to learn the intervention strategies because of the increased cognitive load required to try an unfamiliar interaction with her child plus use new strategies. This is all true. Think back to the mission, though. As early interventionists, we visit families to support learning for both the caregiver and the child. Building on what they already know and do during their daily routine should always be Option 1. There is also value in accessing Option 2, however, which involves suggesting new activities and helping the family create new learning opportunities for the child.

Parenting is all about learning new things, so the key here is a balanced approach. First, ask about, observe, and join routines and activities that already exist for the family, and help the caregiver learn to take advantage of those natural learning opportunities to facilitate the child's development. Second, don't be afraid to introduce and try new ideas after you have explored what the caregiver and child already do. Start with the familiar before introducing new ideas. That sounds easy, but ask any EI practitioner how hard it is to avoid jumping right in with suggestions and you will see lots of heads nodding in the affirmative. Again, it's about balancing your approach. Keep in mind, too, that the caregiver has the ultimate decision-making power about whether she wants to use the new idea, play the new game, or try the new strategy during the visit and between visits. It is this balance between joining what is already happening and respectfully and thoughtfully sharing your expertise to help the family build on what they do and try new things that drives effective intervention.

Pause
and REFLECT
Instructions: Take a breath here to pause and reflect on your practices.

1. How does your work reflect family-centered, capacity-building practices?

_____

_____

_____

2. What challenges do you face with being family centered? With building the capacity of the caregiver to engage his or her child?

_____

_____

_____

3. Which routines and natural learning opportunities have you joined during visits in the past week?

_____

_____

_____

4. Is using a routines-based approach generally easy or challenging for you? Why?

_____

_____

_____

5. When you feel compelled to bring bubbles (or toys, books, etc.) to a visit, what is happening in your work with the family that triggers that compulsion? Who are you bringing the bubbles for—yourself, the caregiver, or the child? This is an important distinction, so take some time to think about it.

_____

_____

_____

6. How could you strengthen your practices to match what you've read so far?

_____

_____

_____

Supporting Caregiver and Child
Learning Through Balanced Intervention

During any intervention visit, there are at least two learners: the caregiver and the child. Both are equally important and both are inextricably intertwined. We will do our best, most effective work when we balance our focus during the visit to ensure that both are learning in the context of interactions with each other. We know that social relationships are the foundation of all learning. Positive social relationships are one of our field's three global child outcomes (Early Childhood Outcomes Center, 2005), meaning that we want all children to have positive social relationships during early childhood because these relationships are important for learning, attachment, communication, getting needs met, and so forth. EI is grounded in the caregiver–child relationship, which is the most important social relationship an infant or toddler has. Whether it is during playtime, when the parent is stretching the child while dressing her in the morning, while running errands, or when a child care provider or grandparent is prompting the child for a /b/ sound during bubble play, these interactions are what facilitate development. If we believe this, then we must consider the importance of caregiver learning as a vehicle through which we enhance child learning. Take a moment to digest this.

If we believe that interactions facilitate development, then we must consider the importance of caregiver learning as a vehicle through which we enhance child learning.

Pause
and REFLECT

If infant and toddler development is grounded in the caregiver–child relationship, what do you believe is your role in promoting development? How do you fit in?

_____

_____

_____

_____

We know that there are some specific intervention practices that facilitate caregiver and child learning. Interventions that help caregivers: 1) identify naturally occurring child learning opportunities and interests that enhance child development (referenced in the mission statement), 2) strengthen caregiver–child relationships and responsiveness to their children, 3) emphasize caregivers' awareness and interpretation of their own actions, and 4) facilitate active caregiver participation, reflection, and decision making have been found to be effective in having a positive impact on child and family outcomes (Bruder, 2010, Dunst et al., 2014; Dunst & Trivette, 2009; Mahoney, 2009; Rush & Shelden, 2020; Swanson et al., 2011). Let's consider each of these and what they look like when integrated into your intervention practice.

Intervention 1: Identify Naturally Occurring Child Learning Opportunities and Interests That Enhance Child Development

The first thing to remember here is that implementing this intervention means that you are helping the caregiver identify these natural learning opportunities and interests. You may be a rock star at identifying them (because that is your job), but this intervention challenges you to take what you can do to a deeper level. You will be sharing your knowledge of how to look for and seize opportunities that occur naturally during the day. You may be able to join lunchtime and spot the opportunity for the child to practice sorting using the veggies and pretzels on the high chair tray, but the caregiver, who is likely more focused on getting food into his squirmy toddler, may not recognize it. You can help the caregiver see the opportunity, think about and prepare to seize it, and then walk through the motions of offering the learning opportunity to the child. You can model what comes next (giving the child the veggies and pretzels in a small pile and then asking him to sort them into two separate bowls). Or you can coach the caregiver by talking about the steps of the activity and encouraging him to think about how he would like to tackle it. Maybe you come up with the idea, but the caregiver knows how the child likes to play, so offers his hands as the vessels the child will sort the food into. Or, perhaps the caregiver could take the idea and get the child to help prepare the meal, sorting foods onto plates for the child and a sibling. By identifying the opportunity and working together on how to seize it, you are building the capacity of the caregiver to notice similar opportunities and take advantage of them in the future. This kind of intervention has the potential to expand the child's learning opportunities well beyond the visit and even beyond that one routine, which is our ultimate aim.

Pause
and REFLECT

How you have implemented Intervention 1 on a past visit? How could you implement it on an upcoming visit? Be specific and describe what you did (or plan to do), what the caregiver did (or what you hope he or she will do), and what the outcome of the intervention was (or will be).

_____

_____

_____

_____

_____

Intervention 2: Strengthen Caregiver–Child Relationships and Responsiveness to Their Children

Interactions that occur during mealtimes and other daily routines are part of what build the caregiver–child relationship. Responsiveness during these routines is essential so that children feel supported in learning things that may be hard for them to do. Children need adults to read their cues, step in and help when needed, provide just the right amount of support, and hang back when appropriate so they can overcome healthy struggles and feel successful. For some caregivers, responsiveness comes naturally and they are very in tune with the child's emotions, means of communication, and daily needs. Other caregivers struggle, especially when there is a history of attachment issues or when the child's ability to communicate, express emotions, and get needs met is difficult to decipher or different from what the caregiver expects. For instance, a child with significant sensory disabilities may communicate in ways that take more time and effort to recognize and understand. As an EI practitioner, you can be pivotal in helping the caregiver identify the child's cues and respond appropriately. The more responsive the caregiver is, the more likely the child will feel safe, confident, and be able to regulate his or her emotions and get his or her needs met (Mahoney, 2009).

Building intervention on responsive relationships is really another key concept for successful intervention. This applies to caregivers other than parents as well. We want child care providers, preschool teachers, grandparents, and others who interact with the child to know how to help the child feel secure and loved. We want these caregivers to know how to facilitate the child's development so that intervention can happen any time an opportunity arises, and the child can generalize what he or she is learning.

> When a child can successfully communicate, problem-solve, or move about in a variety of places with different people during different activities, that is when we know intervention is working.

Pause
and REFLECT   Think of a parent you supported who struggled to be responsive or relate to his or her child. How did you feel while working with this parent and child? What strategies did you use to try to promote responsiveness and relationship building?

_____

_____

_____

_____

Intervention 3: Emphasize Caregivers' Awareness and Interpretation of Their Own Actions

This intervention takes what we do from the surface, where we dole out suggestions and hope one fits ("Have you tried. . .?"), to a deeper level where we are intentional about facilitating the caregiver's awareness of what she does and how she does it. We use reflection and feedback as teaching tools to help the caregiver think about her interactions and activities and the impact they have on the child's development. We help the caregiver interpret what she observes in herself and her child and look for connections so she learns not only what strategies to use but how to use them, why they are important, and what to look for to know if they are effective.

Joyce and Showers (2002), experts in adult education, suggested that gaining a deeper understanding of what was being learned was necessary for an adult learner to generalize and apply that learning across contexts. If you think about it, EI is all about generalization (although we don't call it that with families). We want families to learn intervention strategies and be able to use them with their children whenever and wherever natural learning opportunities occur. When we work with a father to help him practice positioning his son to build trunk control in the stroller, we ultimately want the father to be able to use similar strategies to position his son in the high chair at breakfast, while hanging out at the ball field with his son on his lap, or during any other routine when the child needs to sit upright. Through modeling (when needed) and practice (always needed), we facilitate the father's learning about how to support his son using his hands, towel rolls, or whatever is available. Reflection and feedback help the father learn to recognize what he is doing or could be doing to help his son learn to sit upright. One way to achieve this kind of awareness and generalization would be to practice with the father during the visit and then discuss other opportunities to use the strategies during the week. Or, better yet, we could join the father and child during breakfast or on a trip to the ball field on a future visit to help him use the skills he learned in these different contexts. If we apply Joyce and Showers' suggestion, then it would stand to reason that this father, and other caregivers like him, would find generalization of intervention across daily activities and routines easier if he had a deeper understanding of what to do and how to do it. Your presence and support can help him get there.

Pause
and REFLECT
Imagine that you are working with this father and son to address trunk control during the breakfast routine. The father places his son in the high chair and then squishes a small pillow down into the seat next to his son's right side. The child begins to lean over to the left. What could you say in this moment to encourage the father's awareness and interpretation of the action he took to support his son's trunk? (Tip: Resist the urge to directly point out what you see and think about how you could facilitate the father's thinking.)

Turn to page 163 for sample answers.

Intervention 4: Facilitate Active Caregiver Participation, Reflection, and Decision Making

All of our examples so far have highlighted active caregiver participation, which is fundamental for best outcomes anytime an adult is learning something new. I'd like to shift your perception of the caregivers with whom you work for a moment. Rather than thinking about them primarily in the categories of "parents" or "child care providers," think about them as adult learners. You will learn lots more about adult learning principles and strategies in Chapter 3, so for now, I ask you to start entertaining, and maybe even embracing, the idea that you are a facilitator of adult learning.

Let's step out of the home and into the world of professional development (i.e., training for adults). Research on what is most effective when teaching adults for the purpose of changing their practices indicates that the two most important characteristics of an effective learning experience are *active participation* and *reflection* (Dunst, 2015; Trivette et al., 2009). If you think about it, I have mentioned both characteristics quite a bit already in the context of EI. That is because adults (aka, most caregivers) learn best when they have the opportunity to actively engage with what they are learning by trying it out, applying the information in context, and going through the motions to see how it feels.

Active Participation

Now, picture what happens on many intervention visits: you sit on the floor and play with the child while the caregiver watches. Hopefully, the caregiver is there with you and is part of the interaction, but it's likely that many caregivers still spend a lot of time in a passive observer role. Yes, many of us learn by observation (thank goodness for YouTube), but if you really want that learning to stick, you must do something with what you observed (which is what you do after you watch that YouTube video). Our challenge, then, is in thinking about how to facilitate the caregiver's engagement as an adult learner. How do we help the caregiver "do something" with what he or she is learning? Maybe you invite the caregiver to join an interactive game with the child. You model a playful interaction using an intervention strategy first and then turn it over to the caregiver to try the same strategy. Or, perhaps you never make it to the floor and, instead, join the caregiver and child in whatever they want to do or would have been doing if you were not there. You join in their routine, where the caregiver and child are already engaged with each other and look for those natural learning opportunities for using intervention strategies to encourage development. Sounds easy, right? I know it is not easy in every situation, but I firmly believe that if you enter each home with this perspective guiding you—that you want to find ways to encourage active participation and learning for the caregiver too—then you have taken a huge step toward recommended practice.

> Think of EI visits as practice sessions for the caregiver and
> child with ample opportunities for reflection.

Reflection

Let's think about the other half of that important combo for effective adult learning: reflection. I like to think of EI visits as practice sessions for the caregiver and child with ample opportunities for reflection. The importance of reflection has been recognized in several of our field's most popular intervention approaches. In the early childhood coaching approach, Rush and Shelden (2020) always include reflection with any opportunity to practice. Reflection is also an important component of the Family-Guided Routines-Based Intervention (FGRBI) approach (Friedman et al., 2012). During and/or after a practice episode, you can help caregivers reflect on what they did, what went well, what they would like to change, and how to do that. Active participation helps caregivers apply what was being learned, which may be a new strategy you introduced and modeled. Reflection helps caregivers gain a deeper understanding of what they did by building awareness of their own actions, interpreting those actions in the context of responsive interactions with the child, and identifying the natural learning opportunities during which the strategy could be used next time. Implementing this last evidence-based intervention is intertwined with the other three interventions—they all work together.

Decision Making

Along with active participation and reflection comes decision-making power. Respecting caregivers as key decision makers is an important component of family-centered practice. With that said, how a caregiver chooses to participate and what this looks like will vary from family to family. You may also notice differences across cultures with how family decisions are made and who acts as the primary decision maker. Ultimately, it is each family's decision about what to do with the information we provide, which strategies to use, how and when to implement them, and what routines to share with us for intervention. We will never know as much as the parent about the child and the family's daily life. We want parents and other caregivers to be honest with us about their questions and decisions so that we can share our expertise in ways that help them adapt intervention strategies to fit their lives. If we provide good information, make a safe space for caregivers to feel comfortable (and express their discomfort) with trying out intervention strategies within a supportive, respectful partnership, then we are more likely to facilitate active participation and reflection. If any of these things are not in place—we aren't clear when sharing our observations, ideas, or feedback, we haven't established a comfortable rapport, we don't show respect for what is already happening, we aren't supportive of caregiver decisions— then it will be harder for the caregiver to participate and harder still for us to do our jobs. Let's make it as easy as possible for caregivers to be partners on the EI team, because when we are successful working side by side, everyone benefits and, ultimately, family quality of life improves. What's better than that?

If we provide good information, make a safe space for parents to feel comfortable with trying out intervention strategies within a supportive, respectful partnership, then we are more likely to facilitate active participation and reflection.

Pause
to PRACTICE

Instructions: Read the examples below and check which intervention is being implemented. Hint: Some examples include multiple interventions because when you do this well, effective interventions support one another.

	Intervention 1: Identify natural learning opportunities	Intervention 2: Strengthen parent–child relationships and responsiveness	Intervention 3: Emphasize caregiver awareness and interpretation	Intervention 4: Facilitate active participation, reflection, and decision making
Suki coaches Lexi's grandmother as they pause on the porch swing so Lexi can practice signing to get her grandmother to continue swinging.				
Janika points out when Silas looks at a toy and helps his child care provider recognize that this is how Silas is letting her know his preference for play.				

(continued)

Sarah joins Akeno and his mother at the community pool to help identify ways for Akeno to work his muscles while they enjoy the water.				
Alex reflects with Darcy's father about how when he offered the spoon to her left versus her right side, she seemed to find it more easily in her visual field.				

Turn to page 163 to compare your answers with mine and read an important note about assessing activities against the four interventions.

IMPLEMENTING THE FUNDAMENTALS OF EARLY INTERVENTION: A DOSE OF REALITY

You have just finished reading a refresher on the mission of EI, fundamentals, and evidence-based interventions. This is a good place to take a break, mull over what you've read, and let reality sink in a bit. While you were reading, or perhaps during your next few visits, it might occur to you that while you know *what* to do, actually *doing* it can be hard. Reading about the field's mission or studying recommended practices only goes so far. Understanding these ideas, and even wholeheartedly believing in them, can be very different from implementing them. In fact, when researchers ask practitioners about their knowledge and implementation of recommended EI practices, we are usually quite confident that we know them; however, when those same researchers observe our visits, they find that what we know does not always match what we do. Let's consider why.

EI is a unique, wonderful, and—let's face it—challenging field. We have opportunities to work with many different families in different environments for different reasons. As an EI practitioner, you must take what you know and constantly adapt it to meet the needs of adult and child learners using materials and activities that vary significantly from home to home, and from child care classroom to playgroup setting. You have very little control of the variables in the environment. Because we do not take toy bags into the home anymore, you are not able to control what happens during the visit. Flexibility is a requirement, as is the ability to think on your feet. You join routines during which you are the party who knows the least about what is going to happen. You leave your judgments at the door and maintain an open mind so that you can notice natural learning opportunities, no matter how brief. You share your expertise, knowledge, and experience that took you years to acquire, in 45- to 60-minute sessions with families. You find yourself in situations that are energizing, frustrating, scary, heartbreaking, and heartwarming. On top of that, you work with infants and toddlers who change from visit to visit and who require your compassion, playfulness, sensitivity, and problem solving. They do not always cooperate.

They make you laugh and sometimes make you want to cry. You get up and down off the floor all day and manage the aches that come along with that. You get bitten and spit up on by pets and toddlers, get lost on the way to assessments, take work home with you, and think about families on your days off. This work is hard and it can be messy. All of these intellectual, emotional, and physical aspects of this work are what make it hard to implement the mission of EI with fidelity with every family. That, however, does not mean that we don't try. None of us is perfect, nor are there any perfect EI practices. The important thing here is to be honest with yourself about your strengths and where you need to grow. Reflecting on how consistently you follow the mission of EI and apply the fundamentals is a great place to begin.

> ❝
>
> ## THROUGH PRACTICE, GENTLY AND GRADUALLY WE CAN COLLECT OURSELVES AND LEARN HOW TO BE MORE FULLY WITH WHAT WE DO.
>
> ❞
>
> —Jack Kornfield

Reflective Journal

Instructions: Use this space to capture your thoughts about what you learned in Chapter 2.

NEW IDEAS: _____

_____

_____

_____

_____

_____

IDEAS THAT CHALLENGED ME: _____

_____

_____

_____

_____

_____

_____

THOUGHTS & FEELINGS: _____

_____

_____

_____

_____

_____

_____

Action Plan

Instructions: Based on your reflections in this chapter, what do you want to do next? When you complete your action plan, come back and celebrate it here.

By _____ (date),

I will take responsibility for implementing the fundamentals of early intervention (EI) by _____

_____ (action)

(action examples: balancing my focus on the caregiver and child, embedding more capacity-building into my visits, joining a new family routine, etc.)

ACTION PLAN COMPLETED ☐

My key takeaway: _____

_____

_____

TIPS:

- Review this chapter before your next visit. Jot down a few notes about your goals for the visit as they relate to the four interventions. After the visit, circle back to your notes and reflect on how your practices matched or didn't match with what you intended. Set a goal for the next visit based on what you want to do again or do better.

- Call a team member and discuss a recent visit, keeping what you learned in this chapter in mind. Share any challenges and problem-solve together to help you get closer to best practice.

- Draw a picture of what a visit looks like when it meets the mission of EI. Keep this drawing handy as you reflect on your action plan.

"

BALANCE IS NOT SOMETHING YOU FIND, IT'S SOMETHING YOU CREATE.

"

—Jana Kingsford

CHAPTER
3

~~

Balanced Intervention

Supporting the Caregiver and the Child

s I mentioned in Chapter 2, every intervention visit has at least two learners. When you implement the mission and the fundamentals of EI, you are striking an important balance with your practices between facilitating learning for both the caregiver and the child. Imagine the focus of your EI practices on a balance scale like the one in Figure 3.1.

Implementing the mission means that you understand your role as a guide and coach to the family, affecting the child's development through the interactions between the caregiver and the child. This is an important distinction. You are no longer simply a pediatric therapist, an early childhood/special educator, or a developmental specialist. You no longer focus primarily on what you can do with the child in 45–60 minutes a week. You are a facilitator of learning for children and adults. Wow! Take a moment to let that soak in.

Implementing balanced intervention requires you to find ways to balance your time, your energy, and the support you provide so that both learners are engaged and learning

Child   Caregiver

FIGURE 3.1. Balanced focus.

during the visit. There really is no perfect balance; that is never the expectation. Balancing your intervention approach is more of a perspective, a commitment you make to be intentional about what you do during intervention visits. Your scale will teeter up and down on either side as you offer the child and the caregiver opportunities to explore and use what they know, build on what they already do, and learn and practice new ways of thinking and new interactions designed to encourage healthy development. Sometimes, you will focus more on the child when you try out an intervention strategy, or model it for the caregiver. Other times, you will shift your focus more completely to the caregiver as you reflect and problem-solve together about the use of a strategy or how to overcome a challenging routine. The important thing here is to embrace the balance and understand that the intervention you provide will be much richer and far more effective if you facilitate the adult's learning as well.

> Implementing balanced intervention requires you to find ways to balance your time, your energy, and the support you provide so that both learners are engaged and learning during the visit.

For many of us in early childhood fields, facilitating child learning comes easy. We learned about how to promote child development in college. We learned about effective intervention strategies and recommended practices that we could use with young children and practiced implementing them during our practicum experiences, internships, and clinical rotations. Then we entered the world of EI and found out that we are not only intervening with children, but we must also help their caregivers learn what to do. Here is where we may have veered into less familiar waters.

Supporting learning for adults is often not something we know as much about. Because of this lack of knowledge, we have traditionally resorted to intervention approaches where we focus on the child (so that side of the scale lowers) while the caregiver observes us, so our focus on the caregiver's learning is much lighter (that side of the scale rises) (Salisbury et al., 2010). We've done EI for years with an unbalanced approach and, frankly, it was not "bad" intervention. A more child-focused approach is just a more traditional intervention that is grounded in educational or therapeutic models that reflect a student–teacher or patient–clinician dyad. What we know now is that we can make a bigger difference when we integrate the caregiver more intentionally into the support we provide, creating a triad that includes you, the caregiver, and the child (Salisbury & Cushing, 2013). When support is provided in the context of this triad and is situated in family routines, intervention expands beyond our visit and is sprinkled through the rest of the week when most interactions and learning opportunities for the child happen. The more collaborative the relationship between you and the caregiver, the more likely that the caregiver will feel less stress, more competent about how to help the child, and more confident about family-centered services (Broggi & Sabatelli, 2010). A wise mother I interviewed years ago summed up why this is so important:

The goal is for them to show me what I can do with my child during the week when they're not here. The idea is not for them to come in and do therapy with my child and leave and my child has done his therapy. It doesn't really work that way because an hour a week or an hour twice a week is just not going to work. So, the goal is to help educate me on how I can continue to do that day after day after day….
(VEIPD Videos, 2015, July 31)

This chapter is designed to help you develop your own balanced approach to early intervention. First, we'll consider the EI triad and how you fit with those two other learners, because EI is not just about them—you also play a pivotal role. Next, we will dig into six adult learning principles and think about how they specifically apply to caregiver support in your EI practice. To help you connect the theory to your work, I'll provide you with strategies you can use when engaging both learners during visits. Along the way, you will have lots of opportunities to reflect on what you do now and how you want to grow. To begin, I encourage you to challenge your thinking and set an intention that everything you do as an EI practitioner will consider both learners going forward. Put your intention in your own words.

Pause and REFLECT

My intention for my EI practice is: _____

_____

_____

_____

Ready? Here we go.

THE EARLY INTERVENTION TRIAD

Triad seems like a lovely piece of EI jargon (and we do love our jargon in EI). Usually, I am not a fan of jargon because anything you say with jargon can also be said with more common language. In this case, however, *triad* works well because a single word represents the interactions on any balanced EI visit. The triad includes you, the child, and the caregiver, like this:

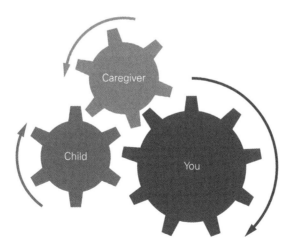

FIGURE 3.2. The balanced early intervention triad.

Because there is always a caregiver learner and a child learner in every visit, we want to do our best to engage them both. Think of the EI triad as a combination of three gears that interlock and affect each other. The interlocking mechanisms represent the interactions the three of you will have. When two gears interlock and turn, they affect the other gear.

That's how the EI support you provide affects the caregiver and the child. When you interact with the child, you do so for dual purposes: to promote the child's development by intentionally showing the caregiver how to use an intervention strategy. When you interact with the caregiver, you do so to build his or her capacity to think about and use intervention strategies in daily routines with the child. When you interact with either learner to practice an intervention strategy, you include the other one. This is important because research suggests that parent-implemented intervention that focuses on supporting parent–child interactions can be very effective (Brown & Woods, 2015). For example, if you engage the child to model how to help him stand on flat feet instead of up on his toes, you talk about what you are doing and why while the caregiver observes. You discuss where you are placing your hands on the child's hips and how you are gently applying pressure to guide the child to his flat feet. Then, you trade places with the caregiver so that she can use the same strategy while you sit nearby to provide guidance and support. You reflect together about how that worked (or didn't work) and how it felt to the caregiver, then plan for how the caregiver can practice using the strategy with the child between visits. It's an active process during which gears are turning and learning is happening for both the caregiver and the child.

Let's contrast this with a more typical approach to EI, which might look something like this:

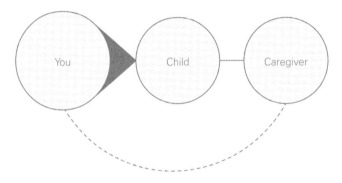

FIGURE 3.3.   The typical early intervention triad.

Here, we have an approach where, as M'Lisa Shelden, coauthor of *The Early Childhood Coaching Handbook* says, you are the main event (Rush & Shelden, 2011). You are the expert and you are there to work with the child. You more directly interact with the child during the visit because he or she is the focus of your attention. After all, you went to school to learn how to educate or "do therapy" with children. You know the caregiver and child are directly linked because, as we often say, "the parent is the child's best teacher." However, because of your focus on the child, your interactions with the caregiver are more peripheral. You engage the child with intervention strategies while the caregiver is present and observing but not necessarily participating or practicing. With this approach, you are most likely telling yourself that you are doing lots of modeling, but in reality you are focusing on the child and hoping the caregiver is taking it in and can replicate what he or she sees you do (again, hopeful modeling). With this traditional approach, the caregiver is a passive learner, if she sees her role in intervention at all. In this situation, it will be more difficult for the caregiver to use intervention strategies she saw you use because there is little to no emphasis on helping the caregiver learn them. If the caregiver does not feel confident using the intervention strategies, then how will interaction and intervention happen between visits? That's really the big question, isn't it?

Pause

and REFLECT   *Instructions:* Think of three recent intervention visits. Use the spaces that follow to reflect on whether your practices tended to be more traditional or triadic. Ask yourself why and be honest so you can recognize what you bring to the visit and the relationship that could be setting the tone one way or another, especially if you find you trend more toward traditional practices. Remember, there is no judgment here; just be honest with yourself.

VISIT #1	VISIT #2	VISIT #3
Description:	Description:	Description:
❐ Traditional ❐ Triadic	❐ Traditional ❐ Triadic	❐ Traditional ❐ Triadic
Why? *What did the caregiver do/not do that contributed to how the visit worked?* *What did YOU do/not do?*	Why? *What did the caregiver do/not do that contributed to how the visit worked?* *What did YOU do/not do?*	Why? *What did the caregiver do/not do that contributed to how the visit worked?* *What did YOU do/not do?*
How could *you* move the visit toward a more balanced approach? What is one thing you could do differently?	How could *you* move the visit toward a more balanced approach? What is one thing you could do differently?	How could *you* move the visit toward a more balanced approach? What is one thing you could do differently?

Now, review all three visit summaries. What patterns do you notice? Did you spend more energy writing about what the caregiver did or did not do? If you trended toward more traditional visits, are the practices you used to conduct all three visits very similar? Did the last question stump you? If you answered *yes* to any of these, then take a deep breath and plan to come back here later after you have learned a strategy or two you would like to try with these families to help bring balance to your visits.

When you approach EI from a balanced perspective and work within the EI triad, you must be mindful of how you spend your time during the visit. Speaking from experience, it can be so easy to get carried away with engaging the child. Just remember that whenever you engage the child, you want to balance that interaction with one with the caregiver too. I know that will be easier sometimes than others, but remember that you are the only one in the triad who knows what the mission of EI and the fundamentals look like. Do your best to lay a firm foundation in how you want to work together from the beginning, and then stay mindful to maintain the balance on each visit. Here are a few strategies to help you establish and maintain the EI triad:

Set the stage. In FGRBI (Woods, 2019), there is a step called "Setting the Stage." During this step, you explain what EI looks like and help the caregiver understand why it is so important that the two of you work together. You emphasize that you are not coming out to the home (or other setting) to primarily work with the child. You are there to support the caregiver so he or she can learn ways to facilitate development toward the IFSP outcomes that are important to the family. Describe what this looks like. Give an example that relates to how you might address the outcomes together.

Start by observing. Rather than jumping right in with your intervention song and dance (we all have one), ask if you can observe a routine that either goes well or one that is challenging. Start by observing, which puts the caregiver in the driver's seat. It is important to prepare the caregiver for the lead role and ask for permission before observing. Starting with an observation can really set the stage for how you will interact with and support the caregiver and child.

Position yourself mindfully. Be very mindful of where you choose to sit or stand. If you choose to always face the child, then that can create a dyad that leaves the caregiver out. However, if you sit beside the caregiver with the child in front of both of you, this could make it easier to pass the interaction with the child back and forth between the two of you. For example, if you are practicing a stretching technique, you could observe the caregiver's attempt, provide feedback, and easily model if needed. Some providers will sit behind the child who is facing the caregiver, especially when encouraging social skills such as turn-taking or when modeling hand-over-hand support. Just remember to switch places so the caregiver can experience how to support the child too. Your body positioning can either get in the way of the triadic interactions or create the conditions for everyone interacting together.

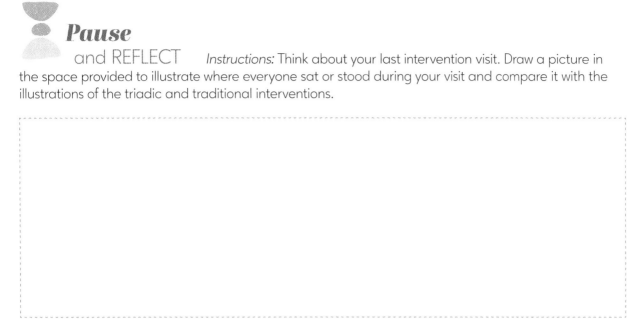

Pause
and REFLECT

Instructions: Think about your last intervention visit. Draw a picture in the space provided to illustrate where everyone sat or stood during your visit and compare it with the illustrations of the triadic and traditional interventions.

On your next visit, pay attention to where you position yourself and whether this facilitates or hinders the balance.

Commit and monitor what you do. Committing to working in an EI triad is the first step. Maintaining it is an ongoing process. You will likely slip back into old patterns, especially in situations where engaging the caregiver is more challenging. When you find yourself interacting with the child for a long period of time, check in about why this is happening. Is it just due to habit? Have you lost the caregiver's attention? In either case, re-engage the caregiver by encouraging her to try the strategy you just used, inviting her to provide feedback, or asking what she would like to do next. If you find yourself drawn into a long conversation with the caregiver and the child has wondered off, do your best to redirect the interaction back to intervention. Ask about what has gone well during the week and what challenges popped up. Ask about progress. Ask what the caregiver would like to work on during that visit. Revisit the plan you made with the caregiver at the last visit and jump back in.

Maintaining the triad can be so easy in some situations and a real challenge in others. Make your commitment and do your best. If you have triadic interactions for 10 minutes on one visit and that's the best you can do, then celebrate and shoot for 11 minutes next time. If the triad works for 45 minutes on another visit, then give yourself a pat on the back and tell a colleague about how well it went. Reflect on what you did and see if there are any techniques that worked well in the 45-minute visit that you could apply to the 10-minute visit. Be gentle with yourself while building your commitment and your own triadic skills. Every visit is different, but your commitment can be the same.

ADULT LEARNING AND EARLY INTERVENTION

An important part of working within the triad is knowing how to facilitate learning for the adult caregiver. I have already mentioned that a passive approach, where the caregiver sits back and watches you, is not the best way to prepare the caregiver for using intervention strategies between visits. Instead, being intentional about encouraging the caregiver's active participation and reflection during the visit will more directly support the caregiver's learning.

Be intentional about encouraging the caregiver's active participation and reflection during the visit.

Recent efforts in the EI field have focused on identifying intervention practices that facilitate learning for the caregiver, who will be responsible for implementing intervention strategies with the child when you are not present (Kemp & Turnbull, 2014; Raab et al., 2010; Rush & Shelden, 2020; Woods & Brown, 2011; Woods et al., 2011). For instance, two of our most important intervention approaches, coaching and routines-based EI, emphasize the caregiver's role as a learner and primary intervention partner with the child (McWilliam, 2010; Rush & Shelden, 2020).

With this in mind, we are going to explore six adult learning principles that can easily be applied to EI practice within the context of the triad. These principles are based on adult learning theory and the work of Malcolm Knowles and his colleagues (Knowles et al., 2012). Knowles is considered the father of andragogy, which according to the dictionary, means "the method and practice of teaching adult learners." Another of my favorite quotes from Woods and Brown (2011) pinpoints why having knowledge about adult learning as an EI practitioner is so important: "Family-centered principles guide practitioners on what to do, and adult learning theory facilitates how to do it."

Linking Adult Learning Theory to Early Intervention

According to Knowles and colleagues (1998, 2012), adult learners are self-directed learners, meaning that they like to have some control over what they learn. They are interested in learning information that is relevant to their needs and are motivated to learn when what they are learning helps them solve problems in their personal or professional lives. To motivate adult learners, it is important to help them understand how learning will be organized, what content they will be learning, why they are learning something, and how it will meet a learning need. Prior knowledge is also important with adult learners. Adults bring their individual prior knowledge and experiences to any learning situation; therefore, learning experiences should respect the adult's prior knowledge and experience and help the learner reflect and build on it.

Pause
and REFLECT   *Instructions:* Take a moment and think about these components of adult learning theory. In your own words, describe how each could be applied in an EI context, then turn to page 164 to compare your answers with mine.

Adult learners like to have some control over what they learn.	
Adults want to learn information that is immediately relevant, solves problems, and meets needs.	

Adults need to understand how learning will occur, what they are being taught, and why it is important.	
Adults bring their prior knowledge and experience to any learning situation.	

It might be tempting to not take a theory too seriously, but many of the key concepts from Knowles's theory have been researched and integrated into the mainstream way we think about learning. In the seminal book, *How People Learn,* by the National Research Council (2000), Bransford and his colleagues summarized the research on learning and teaching and noted that many foundational concepts from learning research apply to both child and adult learners. For instance, they emphasized the importance of being learner centered, developing learning opportunities that are relevant, meaningful, and motivating to the learner. They note that learning opportunities should always describe the knowledge to be shared, why it is important, and what competence looks like. They described the importance of ongoing assessment of learning by the teacher and the learner, which for our purposes in this book will link to facilitating reflection and self-assessment for you and the caregiver. Similar to Knowles's work, Bransford and colleagues also emphasized the pivotal nature of both prior knowledge and context in a learner's ability to retain and use (i.e., transfer) learning in other contexts. This information is essential when considering how to achieve a balanced approach to EI and facilitate learning opportunities that matter to caregivers.

The Overlap Between Caregiver Support and Professional Development

We can also look to professional development research and practice to gain a deeper understanding of what is needed to support our adult learners. Evidence from the adult learning and professional development literature suggests that achieving positive learner outcomes during training requires opportunities for the adult learner to 1) plan for learning, 2) practice and apply what is being learned, and 3) achieve a deep understanding of learned content through reflection and self-assessment (Dunst, 2015; Dunst & Trivette, 2009; Trivette et al., 2009). In their meta-analysis of 79 studies in which adult learning methods were used, Trivette and colleagues (2009) reported that learning opportunities that included all three of these components (i.e., planning, application, and deep understanding) resulted in more positive outcomes for adult learners. That sounds pretty specific to training, and you may have never thought of the work you do with families as training. (In fact, historically there has been resistance to thinking about EI as parent training.) Your work is more of a collaborative, less formal activity, but the idea that you are facilitating learning for an adult is where professional development and caregiver support in EI overlap.

To achieve positive outcomes, caregivers need your help to 1) plan for what they will learn, 2) practice and apply it with their child, and 3) achieve a deeper understanding of what they are learning so they can use it when you are not there.

To help you understand this overlap, let's translate the application of the three components—planning, application, and deep understanding—for use in an EI context. You can provide opportunities for caregivers to help plan for what they want to learn by asking them about what is going well and what is challenging during the day with their child. They can choose routines to focus on, times of day for visits, activities to do during the visit, and how they want to engage their children. Then, you can work together with the caregiver and child in the context of what was planned to help the caregiver apply what he or she is learning. Application might include practice opportunities during visits when the caregiver uses intervention strategies to address the child's development, solve problems, and hopefully help overcome challenges, all with your support. Finally, and this is such an important component, you can facilitate the caregiver's reflection and self-assessment about the practice opportunity so that he or she gains a deeper understanding of what intervention strategy was used, whether or not it worked as intended, why it was important and helpful (or not), and how it could be changed to make it more effective or useful in another routine. Self-assessment can be expanded to include a reciprocal sharing of feedback, too, between you and the caregiver, so that he or she can process the learning experience with your support. Because deeper understanding is needed for learners to successfully generalize what they learn, helping caregivers get to that deeper level of understanding may make it easier for them to take what was learned during the visit and use it during the routines and activities that occur between visits—and remember, that is our ultimate goal.

Based on the work of Knowles, Bransford, and other leaders in EI research and practice (Kretlow & Bartholomew, 2010; Raab et al., 2010; Rush & Shelden, 2020; Trivette et al., 2009; Woods et al., 2011), I have organized six EI adult learning principles that focus on the learning needs of the caregiver. These adult learning principles can be reflected in EI practices that help caregivers 1) learn strategies that are based on family priorities for what is immediately relevant and useful; 2) build on their prior knowledge and experience as the foundation for intervention; 3) understand specifically what to do, why it is important, and how to use intervention strategies with their children; 4) actively participate in the learning process during visits; 5) practice what is being learned in context and in real time during natural routines, activities, and intervention; and 6) reflect and receive feedback on their learning and performance during supportive interactions with service providers (Childress, 2015, 2017). Let's look at each of these six principles and think about how you can connect them to the support you provide to caregivers.

EI Adult Learning Principle 1: Caregivers Learn Best When What Is Being Learned Is Immediately Relevant and Useful

As I've already mentioned, adult learners are self-directed learners, preferring to participate in choosing what to learn and how to learn it (Knowles et al., 2012). By having conversations with families about their priorities for their children's development, we can identify what is important to caregivers and use that information to focus intervention. Finding out what is most immediately relevant for the family is essential when developing IFSP outcomes. The outcomes on a child's IFSP should reflect what the caregivers want the child to be able to do, and what caregivers want is often based on a combination of their own priorities and concerns and what they learn about the child's development through the assessment process. This conversation does not just happen at the intake or the first IFSP meeting; it is an ongoing conversation because what is most immediately relevant and useful to the family of an infant or toddler changes over time as the child grows, family dynamics change, progress occurs, and new challenges arise.

It is important to be flexible and open to learning about what is most meaningful to the caregiver on any visit. You might walk in the door expecting to address one outcome but end up needing to shift gears because something else takes precedence. Let's imagine that you think you are visiting with Janeesa's mother to address her daughter's social communication skills, but when you arrive, you find an exhausted family before you. You initiate a conversation about how the caregiver is doing and you find out that Janeesa has been crawling out of her crib every night. Sleep for the entire family has been disturbed all week and Janeesa's mother is struggling to find a solution. Sure, you could try to initiate turn-taking games with Janeesa and her mother to encourage eye contact and engagement, or you could take some time to problem solve with Janeesa's mother and try to identify some strategies that might help. This new conversation could take a few minutes or most of the visit, which can feel uncomfortable for you when your plan for the session shifts. Taking the time to address what is most relevant and useful for the family not only motivates the caregiver to learn, it also builds rapport, helps the caregiver feel respected and heard, and will probably make it easier for her to benefit from other intervention opportunities after her most important need has been addressed.

Pause to PRACTICE

Instructions: Let's imagine what this EI adult learning principle would look like when implemented during a visit. Read the first scenario and the looks like/doesn't look like examples, and then try to come up with your own examples to practice thinking about what implementing this principle would look like (or not look like) for you. Choose a family you support now to make the exercise easier.

Scenario: When she arrives for her visit, Emily checks in with Jackson's mother, Patricia, about their week. She learns that Jackson has been crying during diaper changes because he does not want to lie still. This routine has become a struggle for him and his mom.

What Does This Look Like?	What Does This NOT Look Like?
Emily asks Patricia if she would like help and Patricia agrees. She also asks what the routine would look like to Patricia if it went well. Patricia says she would like for Jackson to be calm during the diaper change. Patricia attempts to change Jackson's diaper while Emily observes. Together, they problem-solve the routine and identify a new strategy to try to help Jackson feel calm, which involves having him choose a book to look at while he lies on the changing table. Patricia talks about the story while Jackson looks at the pictures, distracting him long enough to get the diaper changed. Patricia feels comfortable with the strategy and relieved to have found something to help.	Emily empathizes with Patricia, saying that it sounds really hard to get through diaper changes. She assumes that she knows why Patricia is worried and asks, "Have you tried changing his diaper on the floor so he doesn't fall off of the changing table?" When Patricia says "No," Emily makes another suggestion and then begins playing with Jackson with his shape sorter. Jackson has outcomes on his IFSP related to problem solving and play skills, and she wants to make sure she addresses them during the visit.

In this space, describe a real scenario from a recent visit that you think reflects EI Adult Learning Principle 1. Or, make up a scenario to practice thinking through how to implement the principle.

Your scenario: _____

_____

_____

_____

What Does This Look Like?	What Does This NOT Look Like?

El Adult Learning Principle 2: Caregivers Learn Best When New Knowledge Is Built on Prior Knowledge and Experience

Every learner brings his or her prior knowledge and experience into any learning situation. Because of this, adults naturally compare what they are learning with what they already know. When what an adult is learning matches with what he or she already knows or has experienced, it is easier to store the new information in long-term memory, retrieve it, and use it later (National Research Council, 2000; Shellenberg et al., 2011; van Kesteren et al., 2014). When the new information does not match or is contradicted by prior knowledge or experience, learning may take longer or require more effort. This can have an important impact on the caregiver–service provider collaboration.

Working in the EI triad requires a close collaboration between you and the caregiver, so understanding what he or she brings to the situation is important. If you understand what the caregiver already knows or has already tried when addressing an IFSP outcome, you will be more likely to develop meaningful intervention strategies. Otherwise, without this information, you might be throwing strategies at the wall (the caregiver and child) and hoping something will stick. I think of this as the "Have you tried . . .?" syndrome (which you saw Emily use in the Principle 1 practice example). I am not opposed to making suggestions to families and, in fact, I think that's an essential part of what we do. However, if we take the time to explore prior knowledge and experience first, we will be less likely to waste time guessing and can use what we learn to identify strategies that may be a better fit for the family.

Pause
to PRACTICE   *Instructions:* Let's imagine what this EI adult learning principle would look like when implemented during a visit. Again, I have provided you with examples below. Keep thinking about the same family you chose for implementing Principle 1, or choose a new family.

Scenario: Drew is visiting with Ms. Flora, London's foster mother. They have been working on London's ability to go up and down stairs because London, at 2 1/2 years old, is getting too heavy for Ms. Flora to carry.

What Does This Look Like?	What Does This NOT Look Like?
Drew's first inclination is to suggest that Ms. Flora place London's favorite toy a few steps up the staircase to motivate London to crawl up the stairs, but he pauses to gather information before making his suggestion. Drew asks Ms. Flora about what she thinks might work to motivate London to climb the stairs. Ms. Flora says that she tried putting London on the third stair, thinking she would have to climb up or down eventually, but London just sat there and eventually cried. Ms. Flora says she has also tried putting her favorite stuffed animal on a step above London to get her to climb, but that did not work either. With this information, Drew recognizes that his original suggestion will not be helpful, so he begins brainstorming with Ms. Flora to find a new strategy to try before they practice helping London learn to climb the stairs.	Drew suggests that Ms. Flora place a toy on the steps to motivate London to climb. Ms. Flora says that she has already tried this and it did not work. When that suggestion does not help, Drew picks up London and begins working with her on the stairs. He tries placing her on the steps to see what she will do. Ms. Flora thinks that she could have told him that London will not crawl up or down the steps because she has already tried that too. Rather than speak up again about a strategy that won't work, Ms. Flora sits back and lets Drew "do therapy" because he is the expert.

Now, expand on the scenario you wrote for Principle 1 or describe a new scenario to illustrate how you would implement Principle 2.

Your scenario: _____

_____

_____

_____

What Does This Look Like?	What Does This NOT Look Like?

EI Adult Learning Principle 3: Caregivers Need to Understand What They Are Learning, Why It Is Important, and How to Use It With Their Children

Knowles and colleagues (2012) described a learner's fundamental "need to know" (p. 140). Adults need to know specifically what they are learning and why it is important. It is not enough to suggest or model an intervention strategy that we think will be useful and relevant. We must take the time to explain the strategy, describing the steps we are taking or walking the caregiver through what to do. Bransford et al. (National Research Council, 2000) also recommended that we discuss how we (you and the caregiver) will know when the strategy works or what it might look like when the caregiver feels competent using it.

Let's think about how this applies to modeling, which is a teaching strategy that we use a lot in EI. Rush and Shelden (2020) suggested that whenever we model a strategy for a caregiver, we describe what we will do or what we are doing and invite the caregiver to look for something specific. For example, we might ask the caregiver to watch how the child reacts. Or we could encourage the caregiver to notice where we place our hands while moving a child who is learning to transition from being on hands and knees to sitting upright. This suggestion is a great strategy for helping the caregiver understand what we are doing and why because it gives the caregiver an active role while we model and it facilitates understanding about the use of the intervention strategy. It is also important to make sure the caregiver understands how to use the intervention strategy without our support. Checking for understanding, reflecting after a practice opportunity, and specifically talking through a plan for how to use the strategy between visits or in the context of other routines will help the caregiver process what he or she is learning. Remember, applying this principle is not only about what you say, it is also about how you support the caregiver in thinking about and using what he or she has learned.

Pause
to PRACTICE

Instructions: Implementing this EI adult learning principle may seem obvious, but let's think more about what it looks like and doesn't look like in practice because understanding the difference is important. This is a principle that most of us probably think we already do well. Challenge yourself here to reflect on the examples I provided, and then dig in and ask yourself how confident you are that you met the caregiver's "need to know" what, why, and how on your last visit.

Scenario: Kyril recently noticed that his daughter, Shaia, did not like to touch grass with her palms and seemed to get upset when her hands were messy, like when they had spaghetti for dinner. He mentions this observation to Melanie, the EI service provider, at the end of a visit.

What Does This Look Like?	What Does This NOT Look Like?
Melanie asks for more information about what Kyril noticed about Shaia's sensitivity to touch. Kyril wonders if her sensitivity might be why she is often fussy. Melanie suggests they see what Shaia would do if she is offered different textures during play, such as fingerpainting with paint, playing in dirt or sand, touching different fabrics, squishing playdough, etc. Kyril worries that Shaia might try to eat the paint and the sand if she touches them at all, so they brainstorm and decide to try fingerpainting with whipped cream instead. Melanie explains that increasing the experiences Shaia has with different textures during activities that are fun for her may help her body's sensory system learn to be more comfortable and less reactive to touching things with her palms. Melanie and Kyril talk about how to try painting with whipped cream during the next visit and come up with a plan for using a cookie sheet while Shaia sits in her booster seat at the kitchen table. Kyril also says he will be prepared next time by dressing Shaia in clothing that can be easily cleaned.	Melanie suggests that Kyril squirt some whipped cream or shaving cream on Shaia's highchair tray or a cookie sheet and let her play in it. She says this is a great game to play when toddlers are sensitive to touch. She asks Kyril to try this before the next visit and let her know how it goes. After Melanie leaves, Kyril thinks about the suggestion and is reluctant to try it because he thinks Shaia will either try to eat the shaving cream or cry because she won't want to be messy. To him, this suggestion does not make sense. He wonders why he would intentionally get his daughter messy when she does not like it. When Melanie returns the following week and asks how it went, Kyril feels embarrassed to admit that he did not try the suggestion. Melanie thinks he did not "follow through," so she tries to come up with another idea.

Continue your thinking about the scenario you wrote previously or describe a new example for implementing Principle 3 from your own experience.

Your scenario: _____

_____

_____

_____

What Does This Look Like?	What Does This NOT Look Like?

El Adult Learning Principle 4:
Caregivers Learn Best Through Active Participation and Practice

In their meta-analysis of adult learning methods and effects on learner outcomes, Trivette and colleagues (2009) reported that the most influential element in the learning process was active learner participation. Let's think about how this finding relates to EI practice. Our most common approaches and techniques in EI, including routines-based EI, coaching, FGRBI, participation-based intervention, and NLEP all emphasize the fundamental and active role caregivers play in effective intervention. Researchers have also consistently found that the use of capacity-building practices (by service providers like you) that actively involve caregivers in learning during visits appear to be related to improved caregiver and child outcomes (Bruder, 2010; Dunst et al., 2014; Swanson et al., 2011). That is powerful because it reminds us that we are the spark that ignites active participation and practice, and when we ignite that spark we are more likely to see progress toward child and family goals. Think about it this way—without the caregiver's active participation during visits, the child is less likely to receive intervention between visits when we are not present. Our mission highlights the importance of our work with caregivers who then encourage child development during family activities and routines. Active participation by the caregiver is what connects what happens during visits with what happens during all of the time between visits.

You are the spark that ignites active participation and practice on visits.

Here's the thing—we know this, but caregivers may not. Sure, you will meet families who are ready to participate and learn from your very first visit. They are ready to dive in and embrace their active roles. You will also meet many families who do not know that they are supposed to be active participants. They may view your time with their family through the same lens that they see their physician who engages the child and then turns to the parent with advice on what to do. Or, they might be reluctant to speak up or join the activity because in their culture, you are viewed as the "expert" so it would be considered disrespectful to "interfere." Keep in mind that you set the tone for the EI visit and you teach caregivers about their active roles. We cannot assume that they know. This is why preparing caregivers for active participation in intervention is so important.

So, what does active participation look like? Does it count when the caregiver is actively participating in a lively conversation with you while you play with the child? Yes and no. Active participation that engages the caregiver to brainstorm with you, think about what the child is doing and why, and consider his or her role in the child's development is very useful. If participation stops at the end of that conversation, however, then it is less impactful because of the adult learner's need to do something with what he or she is learning. This is important to reflect on because research by Salisbury, Cambray-Engstrom, and Woods (2012) that included reviews of video recordings of home visits suggested that conversation and information sharing are among the most frequently used coaching strategies. Conversation is essential, but add in some active practice based on that rich conversation and now you've got yourself a caregiver who is actively engaged and learning.

According to Kolb (1984), the father of the experiential learning model, adults learn best through an interaction between content and experience. In fact, he defines learning as "the process whereby knowledge is created through transformation of experience" (p. 38). By intentionally moving from just talking with caregivers about intervention strategies to offering them opportunities to practice using those strategies during visits, with our guidance and support, we use experience to transform learning. Remember, think of EI visits as practice opportunities for both the caregiver and the child. When caregivers actively practice using intervention strategies during the visit, they will be better prepared to be more successful using these same strategies during everyday activities and routines that happen between visits. Active participation and practice for the caregiver and child benefits them both. How you conduct the visit is the key.

> When the caregiver actively practices using intervention strategies during the visit, he or she will be better prepared to be more successful using these same strategies during everyday activities and routines that happen between visits.

Pause
to PRACTICE
Instructions: You know what to do by now. Let's think about what active participation and practice really look like. As you write your own scenario in the table that follows, be careful to reflect on what you would do, rather than focusing on what the caregiver does not do. For instance, it can be easy to think about what participation would not look like because the caregiver is distracted by other children or won't stay in the room. Instead of "shifting blame" to the caregiver, think about your contribution to the triad and what your practices look like or do not look like when attempting to implement this principle.

Scenario: Marti has joined Catherine and her son, Aiden, in their backyard. Marti asks if she can observe what Catherine and Aiden typically do when they play. She watches as Catherine helps Aiden climb up the ladder and sit at the top of the slide. She then notices how Catherine holds Aiden around the waist as he slides down, while she says "Down!" Aiden smiles and toddles back to the ladder to do it all over again.

What Does This Look Like?	What Does This NOT Look Like?
Marti chats with Catherine about how much Aiden likes the slide and invites her to brainstorm about how this activity could be used to encourage Aiden's communication. They discuss strategies they practiced indoors, such as using wait time and prompting Aiden for a simple word or sign before giving him what he wanted. Catherine tries asking Aiden if he wants "Up?" before helping him climb the ladder. She waits a few seconds, prompts him again, and then helps him climb while saying, "I bet you do want up!" Catherine uses a similar strategy to prompt Aiden for the /d/ sound in "down" before helping him slide down. After practicing this a few times, Aidan enthusiastically says "Dow!" while sitting at the top of the slide. Catherine and Marti clap and cheer. Catherine is excited because she says she hadn't thought of using the strategies she'd already learned inside while out here in the backyard. Now that she's felt successful using them and sees how well they worked, she will show her husband when he gets home.	Marti recognizes the opportunity for Aiden to communicate during the slide routine so she asks if she can try something. She steps in and prompts Aiden to say "up" before helping him climb the ladder. While he sits at the top of the slide, she prompts him again to say "down" and "go." Catherine cheers for Aiden while standing nearby. Eventually, Aiden approximates "dow" before he slides, and everyone cheers. Later that afternoon, when the other family members are home and in the backyard, Catherine tries to use the same strategies she saw Marti use but Aiden does not say "dow" as she hoped. She feels disappointed and a bit frustrated, wondering why he would say it for Marti and not for her.

Keep reflecting here by describing how you would implement (or already have implemented) Principle 4.

Your scenario: _____

_____

_____

_____

What Does This Look Like?	What Does This NOT Look Like?

*EI Adult Learning Principle 5: Caregivers
Learn and Remember Best When What They
Are Learning Is Practiced in Context and in Real Time*

This principle also incorporates practice but focuses on where and when that practice occurs. According to Knowles and colleagues (2012), adult learners are typically problem-centered learners who learn best in the context in which they will use the information they are learning. When new information helps them solve a problem or address a real-life situation in their personal or professional lives, adults are more motivated to pay attention and more ready to learn. These concepts link directly to our field's emphasis on joining families during their daily routines and activities. Learning in context and in real time allows the caregiver to receive support during the actual routine or activity, adapt what he or she knows about the routine with what he or she has learned about intervention, and through practice, integrate the use of the strategy into the natural interactions that occur in that context.

Learning in context is best for the child as well (National Research Council, 2000). Rather than practice prompting a child for language while playing with a food puzzle on the floor (I'm guilty as charged), intervention could be better integrated into the family's snack or mealtime routines when the child would actually be motivated to request food. This would also allow the caregiver the opportunity to practice prompting the child using the family's real food options in the context of how the routine actually works (instead of prompting the child for the tomato puzzle piece when the only tomato he sees in his day-to-day life is in ketchup form). It would be even better if the service provider could schedule the visit to coincide with the family's actual snack time or mealtime so that intervention is practiced in real time. When the practice session occurs during the family's typical routine, the caregiver has the opportunity to try the strategy in context, immediately reflect on what went well or what was challenging and why, problem-solve, and try again if the first attempt is not successful—all with your support. You also get the opportunity to observe and provide that support in the context in which the caregiver needs the assistance, which is much more effective than discussing what to do out of context. Unfortunately, according to research conducted by Sawyer and Campbell (2012) with more than 1,500 early interventionists, this is what we often do when a caregiver shares a challenge that occurs outside of the EI visit—we talk about it. Now that you know the importance of context and practicing in real time, you can be more intentional about moving that conversation to a practice opportunity that better facilitates learning for both the caregiver and the child.

Pause
to PRACTICE
Instructions: As you read the following scenario, think about contexts that have been important on your own visits. What routines and activities have you joined? Where have you met the family to practice intervention? Why were those contexts important? If most of your visits have occurred on the living room floor, challenge yourself by imagining a visit with one of the families you support in a different context. Think about how you could address the IFSP outcomes in context and in real time and what a difference this might make for the caregiver and child.

Scenario: When Renee asks how their week has gone, Penny, Luna's aunt, shares that she has been struggling to get Luna to sit in the shopping cart at the grocery store. They typically stop by the store several times a week, and lately they cannot even make it into the store without Luna falling apart. Penny is not sure what to do and asks Renee for help.

What Does This Look Like?	What Does This NOT Look Like?
Renee and Penny talk more about what happens at the store. After about 10 minutes, Renee asks if Penny wants to go to the store now so they can work together to try to figure out what is happening. Penny is surprised that Renee can do that but is excited for the help. They drive to the store and Renee asks to observe what Penny and Luna typically do. Renee watches as Penny gets a shopping cart, then moves Luna from the car directly to the shopping cart seat. She buckles Luna in, locks the car, then begins pushing the cart to the store front. Within a few seconds, Luna begins to cry. Renee shares her observation that Luna seemed fine until the cart started moving across the parking lot. She also noticed that Luna covered her ears when she cried. She asks Penny what she thinks about this and Penny says that putting Luna in the cart out in the parking lot is new. In the past she carried her inside but now that Luna is getting bigger, it's harder to carry her. Penny wonders if the noise of the cart rattling across the asphalt is too loud for Luna. Penny takes Luna out of the seat and hugs her as she calms down while Renee moves the cart back to the cart coral. Renee suggests that Penny try holding Luna's hand while they walk to the store before putting her in a shopping cart seat to avoid the noise. Penny tries this and, although it takes a little longer, she feels like it is a good solution.	Renee asks Penny if she has tried reserving a special set of toys or books to bring to the store for Luna. She also suggests singing to Luna as they move around the store to keep her occupied. Penny says that Luna does fine in the store if they can just get in there; Luna starts crying while they are out in the parking lot. Renee asks if Penny has anyone who can babysit Luna while she does her shopping. Penny sighs and says that she has switched to shopping in the evening when her husband is home, which is hard because it disrupts the family's evening routine. Renee keeps trying to think of helpful ideas, but since she is not sure what the problem really is, it is hard to know how to help.

Now, try to think beyond the living room floor to reflect on other possible contexts for your EI visits. Describe a scenario from experience or make one up based on a recent conversation with a family. Get specific here to stretch your thinking about Principle 5.

Your scenario: _____

_____

_____

_____

What Does This Look Like?	What Does This NOT Look Like?

EI Adult Learning Principle 6: Caregivers Benefit From Opportunities to Reflect and Receive Feedback on Their Learning and Their Performance

Remember the link mentioned earlier that shows the relationship between professional development and the support provided to caregivers? Consider this: Professional development that actively engages adult learners in practice, reflection, and feedback opportunities appears to be associated with better learning outcomes (Church et al., 2010; Dunst et al., 2011; Maturana & Woods, 2012; Penuel et al., 2007; Snyder et al., 2011; Trivette et al., 2009). When we support caregiver learning during visits, we want to achieve "better learning outcomes" too. It appears that families who are more actively engaged during visits through opportunities for reflection, active participation, and feedback reap greater benefits from intervention and are able to provide supports for their children between EI visits (Trivette et al., 2010). Let's think about why reflection and feedback are important.

Reflection is necessary for adult learners to build on what they know, consider options, and evaluate their own mastery and success with using what they learned (National Research Council, 2000; Trivette et al., 2009). We can help caregivers reflect on their interactions with their children, their children's behavior and development, and their own actions by being intentional about the conversations we have. We can use open-ended questions to facilitate reflection so that caregivers think about what they are learning and gain a deeper understanding of how to help their children. For example, instead of telling Penny what to do (in our last scenario), Renee could use a few good open-ended questions to help Penny think through her actions and work toward a solution to the grocery store problem. Renee could ask, "What was happening right before Luna started crying?" or "Has anything recently changed about your trips to the store? What might this be?" Renee would not be holding back information; she would be helping Penny use her own resources to think about the situation. Reflection helps caregivers think about what they do and why they did it, a pattern of thought that they can use in other situations when the service provider is not present (Lorio et al., 2020). That is important because you, like Renee, are typically only with the caregiver for an hour (or less) each week. Helping him or her learn to observe, consider the situation, and problem-solve without you are skills the caregiver can use well beyond the EI visit.

Similarly, feedback provides the adult learner with information he or she can use to evaluate success and problem-solve what to do to get closer to the intended outcome. Specific feedback that describes what the caregiver did or did not do, what the child did, and so on, builds awareness of what went well, how the child reacted, and why the caregiver's actions contributed to the outcome. For example, Renee could have provided informative feedback to Penny if Penny had not wondered about Luna's sensitivity to sound, like this: "Remember how you've said that Luna covers her ears when she hears the vacuum or other loud noises? I noticed that she covered her ears when she started to cry." This example of feedback also fosters reflection by encouraging Penny to think about what she knows. Or, when Penny was initially sharing her frustration about not being able to go to the grocery store with Luna, Renee might have used affirmative feedback, such as "Wow, that must be really hard to not be able to go to the store when you need to," which acknowledges that she heard Penny's concern. What feedback sounds like will depend on the situation. The important thing to remember is to be as specific as possible so that caregivers gain information that will help them learn.

Facilitating reflection and feedback is important when coaching families and is often easy to forget and hard to do. Unfortunately, providing opportunities for caregivers to receive feedback, problem-solve, and reflect on their performance have been found to be underused practices during EI visits (Barton & Fettig, 2013; Salisbury et al., 2012). Facilitating conversations that include reflection and reciprocal feedback can be challenging for us for lots of reasons: our own inexperience conducting visits this way, a lack of rapport with the caregiver, caregivers (and service providers) who are not naturally reflective, our fear of asking for or providing feedback because we aren't sure what to do with what we hear, and so forth. It can take time to develop the skills needed to effectively use reflective questions and provide specific feedback to families, and that's okay. Even if you start with the intention of asking one reflective question or using at least one specific feedback statement on your next visit, you are moving closer to the goal of helping families think about what they do, what they want to do, and how to go about doing it. We want to encourage metacognition in caregivers and help them think about what they think and do. I am not suggesting that caregivers do not already think; instead, I am suggesting that impactful EI encourages a deeper level of thinking about caregiving, which could lead to easier maintenance and generalization beyond the visit. If we want to increase caregiver confidence and competence about how to use intervention strategies with their children, then going deeper using reflection and feedback makes sense.

Pause
to PRACTICE

Instructions: Here is your final scenario. These practice opportunities have offered you opportunities to either reflect on past visits or practice thinking about what you could do. So that you can receive feedback, share your scenarios with a colleague or your supervisor and ask how well they match (or don't match) with the implementation of each EI adult learning principle. The great thing about working through a book like this is you can have a do-over. Use the feedback you receive to tweak your scenarios. Come back and add to them as you practice what you are learning.

Scenario: Xavier's child care provider, Mia, is struggling to find ways to include him during activities when the other children are standing. She talks to his parents and they suggest having their early interventionist, Scott, come to the classroom. Mia agrees and hopes he can help.

What Does This Look Like?	What Does This NOT Look Like?
When Scott arrives, he introduces himself to Mia and chats with her about the classroom and her goals for Xavier. When it is time for the children's activity to change, Scott watches as Mia joins the children at the sand table. He notices that Xavier, who was sitting in the construction area, stays there because he cannot move about yet. Mia notices too and picks up Xavier to bring him to the table. She struggles with how to include Xavier in the activity because he is not yet standing by himself. Scott tells her, "I can see that you are trying to include Xavier but it looks like it's hard because he isn't yet standing." Mia agrees and asks Scott for ideas. He encourages Mia to think about what she has already tried by asking, "How does Xavier participate in other activities, like during art time?" Mia says that sometimes she can get Xavier to stand between her knees at the art table for a few seconds. Scott asks if she could show him how she does that. Mia helps Xavier stand but notices that his legs quickly give out. He asks Mia if Xavier wears his ankle-foot orthoses (AFOs) at child care. Mia does not know what AFOs are, so Scott explains. He finds out that Xavier's parents have sent his AFOs in his backpack but Mia did not know if she should put them on or how to do it. Scott shows Mia how to put on the right AFO then she puts on the left AFO. After putting Xavier's shoes back on, Mia is eager to see how Xavier stands now. She sits at the sand table again with Xavier supported between her knees. Scott asks Mia, "What do you notice about how Xavier is standing now?" Mia notices that Xavier seems much more stable now. She wishes she had known how to put his AFOs on sooner and is delighted that he can participate at the table with his friends.	When Scott arrives, he greets Mia and then sits down with Xavier in the construction area. He chats with Mia until the children move to the sand table to play. Scott carries Xavier to the table and tries to help him stand. He notices that Xavier is not wearing his AFOs so he checks Xavier's cubby. When Mia sees him putting the AFOs on Xavier's feet, she asks what they are. She tells Scott she had seen them in Xavier's backpack but was not sure what to do with them. Scott shows her how to put the AFOs on while explaining how they support Xavier's ankles, where he has low muscle tone. Mia tries to watch Scott and Xavier as he helps Xavier stand at the stand table but she is often distracted by the other children. She and Scott talk about what Xavier likes to do and discuss strategies Mia can try for helping him participate in table activities. Mia is happy to have the ideas but feels unsure about how to get Xavier to stand and even how to put on his AFOs. When Scott leaves, she tries to do what she saw him do but stops when Xavier begins to fidget as if he is uncomfortable. She wishes Scott were there because she is still not sure what to do.

Describe your final scenario here. How did you use reflection and feedback on a past visit to facilitate the caregiver's understanding of the intervention strategy or activity? Or, rewrite what really happened during that visit and imagine what you could do differently next time.

Your scenario: _____

_____

_____

_____

What Does This Look Like?	What Does This NOT Look Like?

Adult learning matters in early intervention. It affects how you support families, what happens on visits, and how confident families are with using strategies they learn between visits when you are not there. Before you read this chapter, you may have recognized that you teach adults. Most likely, you already knew that you were a partner and collaborator with parents and other caregivers. Or maybe you had never thought about how caregivers learn, instead relying on their powers of observation to glean what they needed to know. Wherever you started, consider where you are now. Now you know the importance of balancing some of your energy as a service provider on the learning experience of the caregiver. High-quality EI is always balanced between supporting learning for both the child and the caregiver. Both need learning opportunities during the visit. Both need to practice new skills they are learning. Both need to be actively engaged by the EI practitioner (you) to participate in intervention. Your role is to bring this awareness into the visit and mindfully facilitate interactions that result in learning experiences for both learners. It's all part of the EI balancing act.

EI practice is all about balance. It's a balance between building on what the family already does with their child and developing new ideas. It's a balance between joining the family in their natural routines and activities and helping them create new learning opportunities for the child. It's a balance between focusing on the child's development, which is our reason for being there with the family and facilitating the caregiver's ability to encourage development when we are not there. For us as service providers, it can be a balance between knowing what we can do with children and finding ways to transfer that knowledge and skill to the caregiver. Ultimately, I think EI is a practice that challenges us to balance our intention and our attention between facilitating child and caregiver learning. Before we wrap up this chapter, let's dig into what this means about how we share our expertise and why it matters.

Setting Your Intention and Attention

When you believe in the mission of EI and the fundamentals, which we reviewed in Chapter 2, you have guiding principles on which to set your intention for your EI practice. *Setting your intention* is a phrase that is common in mindfulness and yoga practices. It means being intentional about what you want to do. It's like setting a goal for yourself by priming your mind for action in a certain direction that you chose. (You actually set your first intention at the beginning of this chapter.) With EI practice, you can set your intention to view your role as a coach and guide for the caregiver. You can decide that you will enter every door with the intention of looking for opportunities for both the caregiver and the child to learn. How this plays out may look different with each family but starting from a place of commitment is a first step.

Once you have set your intention, it guides where you focus your attention. It reminds you to keep your attention on what both learners are experiencing. It helps you shift your attention back to the triad so that all three of you are actively participating, which is especially important when you drift into the space where you and the child are working together while the caregiver watches from the sidelines (the drift is real). Setting your intention and monitoring your attention also affect how you share your expertise, an important thing to address because one of the biggest concerns I have heard from practitioners who use coaching and the routines-based model is "Where does my expertise fit in?"

SHARING YOUR EXPERTISE IN BALANCED INTERVENTION

It really is impossible to work in the context of the triad, provide support during family activities, and balance your intention and attention between facilitating learning experiences for the caregiver and the child without sharing your expertise. If you only tag along, watch what families already do, and give them positive feedback about how great they are, you are not sharing your expertise. Coaching, using routines-based EI, using capacity-building practices—all of these approaches require your expertise. Without you sharing what you know, there is no point to EI. What you bring to the triad is your knowledge and experience about child development, family systems, best practices in EI, and how to adapt intervention strategies to address specific needs and activities. Families come to EI because they want you to share what you know. Balanced intervention and a healthy appreciation for adult learning require that you share your expertise by creating an equal partnership that respects the expertise caregivers bring to the table too. You need to know what they know about the child's strengths, interests, and needs. You will provide more meaningful intervention if you now tap into the caregiver's expertise on how the family works, what their daily life is like, and how the child participates (or struggles) in everyday activities. You could never know enough on your own without the family. It takes mutual respect (and perhaps a lowering of the ego for some of us) and a healthy awareness of child and adult learning to realize that balancing the support you provide requires that you share what you know so that both learners are engaged. It's not always easy, but it is well worth the effort.

In the next three chapters, you will learn more about how to implement balanced intervention and how to facilitate caregiver and child learning by gathering meaningful information, conducting balanced intervention visits, and (don't forget this one) taking good care of yourself. I will offer you specific strategies for applying the adult learning principles and opportunities to reflect on your attempts. Take a moment now to pause and process what you have learned so far.

Reflective Journal

Instructions: Use this space to capture your thoughts about what you learned in Chapter 3.

NEW IDEAS: _____

_____

_____

_____

_____

_____

IDEAS THAT CHALLENGED ME: _____

_____

_____

_____

_____

_____

THOUGHTS & FEELINGS: _____

_____

_____

_____

_____

_____

Action Plan

Instructions: Based on your reflections in this chapter, what do you want to do next? You know what to do.

By _____ (date),

I will take responsibility for balancing my approach to early intervention (EI) by _____

_____

(action).

(action examples: balancing focus on child and adult learning, working in the context of the triad, implementing a specific EI adult learning principle, setting my intention and attention, etc.)

ACTION PLAN COMPLETED ☐

My key takeaway: _____

_____

_____

TIPS:

- Choose an EI adult learning principle to focus on each week for the next 6 weeks. Before each visit, think ahead about how you might incorporate that principle into your interactions with the family. During the visit, stay mindful about how opportunities to implement the principle show up. After the visit, reflect here in writing or use a notes or voice recorder app on your mobile device to capture your thoughts about how you used or could have used that principle.

- Share what you are learning about balanced intervention and adult learning with your colleagues at an upcoming staff meeting. Invite them to come up with ideas for how each principle could be implemented during an EI visit at the next meeting, revisit the principles and check in about opportunities in their practice when the principle was or could have been addressed.

- To learn more about the topics covered in this chapter, take the free online course, *Supporting Caregiver Learning During Early Intervention Visits*, on the VA Early Intervention eLearning Center site (https://veipd.org/elearn/). You will find the course under the Ongoing Professional Development Courses list as part of the Effective Practices courses.

"

WHILE IT IS WISE
TO LEARN FROM
EXPERIENCE, IT IS
WISER TO LEARN FROM
THE EXPERIENCES
OF OTHERS.

"

—Rick Warren

CHAPTER
4

Gathering Meaningful Information From Families

Pause and REFLECT   Take a moment to answer the following two questions:

1. What was your happiest moment?

_____

_____

2. What is your greatest fear?

_____

_____

Now, imagine that you must share your answers with a total stranger. Look around you and consider sharing what you wrote with the first person you see. If you are by yourself (which is how I like to read), think about sharing what you wrote with a stranger. You don't know this person, but you need this person to like you and help you. This person has something you need, and you want to make a good impression. You hope that your answers will do that, but you really don't know why you were asked these very personal questions or what this stranger is going to do with your information.

How do you feel right now?

_____

_____

N ow, let's put this exercise in the context of EI. We frequently ask families to share very personal information, often starting with our very first contacts or visits before we really get to know them. We ask for personal information about the mother's pregnancy and the child's delivery, which could for some parents be among their happiest and/or most frightening experiences. We ask about priorities and concerns for their children, which could get very close to the question I asked you about your greatest fear (e.g., "Will my child ever talk?" or "When will she learn to walk?"). We need to know about financial status, resource needs, and how the child and family spend their day. We need a lot of detailed information just to get the ball rolling to determine a child's eligibility, and then we need even more information to develop a meaningful IFSP. Imagine the caregiver's experience and compare it to the exercise that opened this chapter. Think about how you felt—uneasy? anxious? vulnerable? We want to do whatever we can to decrease the distress that can come with sharing information for families while gathering the information we need to prepare for and provide individualized, balanced intervention. Remember EI Adult Learning Principle 3 discussed in Chapter 3? Like caregivers, it is important that you understand why we need to gather good information, so let's start there. Then, we'll think about what kind of information we need and how to gather it in a sensitive, respectful matter, which is equally as important as why we need the information in the first place.

WHY DO WE NEED TO GATHER INFORMATION?

By now, I'm sure you understand the inherent value in treating the caregiver as your EI partner. In this partnership, both of you bring valuable knowledge, certain understandings, and unique experiences that are absolutely essential to supporting the child. You bring your discipline-specific knowledge, an understanding of infant and toddler development and family-centered practices, and knowledge and experience with how to engage young children using intervention strategies that promote development. You also are the member of the partnership who best understands how the EI collaboration should work. The caregiver brings his or her knowledge of family priorities, an understanding of child and family functioning during daily routines, and experience with interacting with the child every day. In order to combine the expertise of both partners, you must be intentional about tapping into what the caregiver knows, understands, and has experienced. You do this through gathering information that will help you understand the child and family and how the three of you (the triad) can work together.

> You must be intentional about tapping into what the caregiver
> knows, understands, and has experienced.

Although this may sound unidirectional, it is not. Because the EI partnership is a reciprocal relationship, whenever you gather information, you are also very likely to provide it. Gathering information is essential at the beginning so we often see the service provider (or service coordinator in some instances) asking more of the questions and the caregiver sharing more information. As the relationship progresses and you have more information on which to base your support, you will move into providing more information that supports caregiver–child intervention. This gathering and giving of information (Woods & Lindeman, 2008) becomes a back-and-forth volley where both sides see each other as resources with something important to share.

WHAT INFORMATION DO WE NEED TO GATHER?

Let's face it. We cannot do our jobs well without information from families. We cannot conduct the evaluation and assessment without input from caregivers about how children interact, behave, and participate in everyday family activities and routines. Yes, some programs still conduct standardized testing of infants and toddlers and make decisions based on these test scores; this is possible, but it leaves out the functional information we need to prepare to work toward the mission of EI. Without functional information about the child's abilities, strengths, and needs in daily life, we risk basing decisions on an infant's or toddler's abilities to cooperate with unfamiliar tasks that may or may not be culturally or practically relevant in his or her daily life (Bronfenbrenner, 1979). Remember that our goal with intervention is to support caregivers' interactions with children so they can promote development during naturally occurring learning opportunities. To do this, we need to gather information about what routines go well and where the struggles are before and during the assessment. This ensures that we can write IFSP outcomes and plan for intervention that addresses both types of routines, in partnership with the caregiver. This starts with a healthy discussion about family priorities that goes deeper than asking, "What are your concerns?"

Information About Family Priorities Versus Concerns

Pause
and REFLECT   *Instructions:* Jot down three sentences to capture what you hear most often when a caregiver is asked "What are your concerns?" Then keep reading to compare what you wrote to what I hear.

1. _____
2. _____
3. _____

When we focus on caregiver concerns, we are likely to hear some of the same things across families:

> "We're worried that he's not talking."

> "She is not doing what her brother was doing at this age."

> "Shouldn't he be walking by now?"

Knowing what the main concerns are is important and in fact we are required by law to ask about them, but I want to suggest that if you focus here, you will only gather surface-level information. Moving the discussion to a deeper level that invites caregivers to consider their priorities for the child requires that you approach the information gathering from a perspective of discovery rather than one where you assume you know what the caregiver means.

It is so easy to assume we know what a parent means when she says she's worried that her 2-year-old isn't talking. We can easily recognize a delay when a toddler only speaks three words because we understand development. What we can't know is the impact this delay is having on the family. Unless we open the door for the caregiver to tell us, we will not know what the caregiver wants the child to be able to do. Sure, in this example we can assume the caregiver wants the child to talk, but what would this look like for the family? How would it make life easier if the child could talk? When during the day would it matter that the child can communicate? This deeper level information is what we need in order to write an IFSP and provide intervention supports that match what is important to families. We need deeper-level information for meaningful intervention.

> We need deeper-level information for meaningful intervention.

In a nutshell, here is the difference between concerns and priorities. Concerns are the reasons children are referred to EI: delays in walking or talking, differences in interactions with others, low muscle tone, difficulties with feeding, and so forth. General concerns like these are typically not very specific, at least at first before we dig into why the child is showing the delay. Priorities, however, are very specific. Priorities flip the concern to focus on what the caregiver would like to see the child be able to do as a result of intervention. What success looks like will be specific for each caregiver. The words they use may be similar, but the vision is unique. Sure, sometimes you might ask a parent about concerns and priorities and get the same answer: "I just want him to talk!" If this happens, take a moment to step back and think about how you asked the question. Here's an example of how you can gather this information about concerns and priorities to get to a deeper level.

> Concerns are the reasons children are referred to EI. Priorities flip the concern to focus on what the caregiver would like to see the child do as a result of intervention.

Example 1: Concerns

Service provider: What are you concerns for Josie's development?

Mother: She whines a lot and only says a few words like "goggie" for doggie and "dat" for that. I think she should be saying more words by now.

In this example, the service provider learned that the mother is worried about expressive communication. He learned that the child is saying a few words, which is very helpful to know. He also learned that the child is whining, which suggests that she is trying to communicate but is not able to. What the provider does not know is what the child needs to be able to say in the context of the family. Sure, if we check our assessment tool, we may know that Josie, as a 25-month-old child, should be saying 50 words by now. We could randomly pick common words to target or bring toys out and attach words to the games we choose to play during intervention visits. Or we could dig into priorities to find out where intervention should really focus for this child and this family.

Example 2: Priorities

Service provider: When you think about how Josie is communicating right now, what would you like her to be able to do? Think about what is important to you. What would you like her to be able to tell you? What would make things easier for you and Josie?

Mother: Well, I want her to talk instead of whine all day.

SP: Instead of whining, what would you like her to say? When she is whining, what do you think she is trying to tell you?

Mother: She whines when she's hungry or tired or can't get what she wants, like when her cup is empty. I'd like her to tell me what she wants. If she could say something like "crackers" or "go outside," or maybe "more" when she's thirsty, that would be a great start.

By helping the mother reflect on her priorities, the service provider has learned deeper-level information that is specific to this family. Ask a different parent whose toddler whines all day and only says a few word approximations and you will probably hear a very different take on priorities because every family works differently. When we gather information that is specific to the family, we begin to better understand and appreciate their strengths and needs. In this scenario, this mother is struggling but still in tune with what her child is trying to communicate. That is a wonderful strength. We learn that she is not just annoyed by her child's whining; she wants to understand her child and recognizes her child's struggle too. We learn information that helps us with an accurate, functional assessment of her child's development. We also learn information that will help the rest of the EI team determine where to start with intervention. IFSP outcomes can be written to address the mother's priorities for her child's communication, and the service provider has a firm place to begin with exploring the routines mentioned in the mother's comment—eating favorite foods (cracker) and joining a favorite activity (going outside). Gathering this kind of information about a caregiver's concerns and priorities (and resources) is required in our federal law; understanding the difference, as I hope you can see here, is essential for effective intervention.

Information That Supports Active Caregiver Participation

Gathering meaningful information from the caregiver not only helps us understand the family and identify where to begin with intervention, it also lays the foundation for the caregiver's active participation. Let's think about Adult Learning Principles 2 and 4. Principle 2 suggests that *caregivers learn best when new knowledge is built on prior knowledge and experience.* By intentionally asking about prior knowledge and experience from our earliest conversations, we are developing relationships with caregivers that demonstrate our respect for what they know. We want caregivers to be actively thinking, brainstorming, sharing information, asking questions, and ultimately using what they know and learn to help their children.

Gathering meaningful information lays the foundation for caregivers' active participation and demonstrates respect for what they know.

These early and ongoing conversations promote active participation, which according to Principle 4 is essential for caregiver learning. Of course, implementing these principles when gathering information must also include Principle 3 so that caregivers understand why you are asking questions and gathering information. Just being asked personal questions without an understanding of why they are important can backfire and feel intrusive. Always be sure to explain why you need to ask a question, why it might be important, and how the information will be used. Give the parent permission to decline to answer; making choices about how to participate is also part of Principle 4. Just remember, how we gather that information is as important as what we ask about so be sure to do it respectfully and kindly to show that you value what the caregiver contributes to the intervention partnership.

Information About the Child's Development

We ask caregivers a lot of questions about their children. We ask about the child's prenatal health, birth, and postnatal status. We ask about medical history and developmental milestones. During the developmental screening (if conducted), evaluation, and assessment, we often rapid-fire questions at the caregivers about the child's eating, sleeping, pooping, crawling, walking, playing, dressing, communicating, interacting . . . Do you feel overwhelmed yet? It's a lot to ask, especially during a process that is probably new and foreign to the caregiver. It's a lot to share when the caregiver may be feeling nervous and vulnerable because strangers are asking questions about the most precious person in the world to that caregiver, questions that caregivers sometimes don't know the answer to. Most parents find themselves immersed in their child's day-to-day life because of the demands of caring for an infant or toddler, so talking about the child may come naturally. For others, answering questions about development may call attention to deep-seated fears about the child's development or fresh wounds the caregiver may be feeling after a recent diagnosis. We must find ways to gather developmental information in a conversational manner that gives the caregiver permission to share as much or as little as he or she is comfortable sharing. How we gather this information requires skill on our part.

HOW TO GATHER MEANINGFUL INFORMATION FROM FAMILIES

The skills you need to gather meaningful information are not always learned in college courses or during onboarding after hire. Even if they are taught early on, practicing these skills in a real-world context is necessary for you to really learn them. Of course, good communication skills are essential, but you also need skills that make information gathering more successful, such as building rapport, preparing for information sharing; developing relationships; having rich, respectful conversations; and closing communication loops so that our communication partners know what comes next. Think of gathering information as a cycle (Figure 4.1) rather than a link between two people:

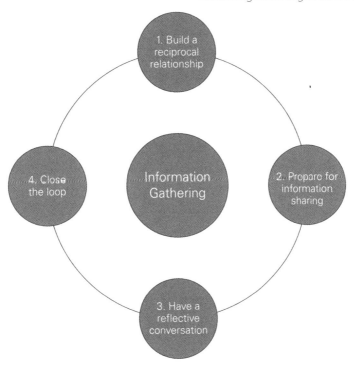

FIGURE 4.1. The information gathering cycle.

Let's consider the skills along this cycle and why each is important.

Skill 1: Build a Reciprocal Relationship

Information gathering begins at our very first contacts with families, before we have had much time to build rapport or get to know the family. That is just the nature of the EI process, which is bound by federal and state timelines. We have to jump in feet first and take families along with us. For service coordinators who conduct intake visits, they may have 1–2 hours to meet a family, begin to get to know them, gather initial information, and complete required documentation to start the eligibility process. For service providers, you might meet the family for the first time at the assessment or later during your first intervention visit. In any case, you can be intentional about taking time to establish positive rapport and begin to build the relationship on which your partnership will stand. This relationship is also key to the intervention triad and requires ongoing nurturing. Here are a few strategies for establishing and nurturing a reciprocal, respectful relationship:

> Be intentional about taking time to establish positive rapport and begin to build the relationship on which your partnership will stand.

Dedicate time to relationship building. Relationships are built on shared information, spending time together, and building connection. A great place to begin is by making the first 5–10 minutes of every visit a time to simply chat with the family. Ask how they are and how their week has gone, and then actively listen. Revisit priorities and plans previously mentioned. Listen for things the caregiver shares that allow you to make connections:

"You're a big sports fan? Me too!" or "Oh, you like to go to the beach? What does Elijah think of the sand and the waves?" Connections can build rapport and help the caregiver feel more comfortable with sharing information with you. They also help you understand the child and family. Whatever the caregiver chooses to share, be sure to use your body language to show your interest and provide kind, attentive feedback: "That sounds really hard. Is that something you would like us to address?" If you are early in your relationship, it can be helpful to look for opportunities to compliment the family too: "Wow, you have so many beautiful plants. Does it take a lot of time to care for them?" Sure, asking about plants might not provide you with information you can use to write the IFSP, but showing interest can lay a foundation for the caregiver to see that what is important to her matters to you. Or, like I once did, asking about the plants could lead you to find out that the child is learning to help with watering. This simple plant-watering routine offered natural learning opportunities I might not have known about if I had not paid the compliment. The time you take for relationship building is never wasted time because, as Tomlin and Viehweg (2016, p. 3) said, "Relationships of all kinds matter because we learn best through them."

Share something about yourself (within professional boundaries). Sharing information about yourself can be an effective way to build that reciprocal relationship that is essential to EI. You might consider sharing information about some of your interests if they relate to family interests. Or perhaps you and the caregiver grew up in the same area of the state. When you choose to share information about yourself, be sure that it serves the relationship you are building in the context of EI and does not cross professional boundaries. This can be a very fine line. Relationship building in a professional context means that you are friendly with the caregiver but not entering into a friendship. Sharing too much personal information can make caregivers uncomfortable, such as talking about the argument you had with your partner last night or sharing your child's milestones when the caregiver's child is far away from those accomplishments. I learned this lesson the hard way when my son was the same age as the child I was working with. The mother and I would chat about our children and she would frequently ask about my son. During one visit, I remember mentioning that my son was "talking up a storm." Her face changed as she said how wonderful that was and I could detect that my inadvertent "mommy moment" had reminded her what her son was not yet doing. This was definitely not my intention but still did damage. It was a reflection point for me to realize that I was crossing a boundary that was not serving either of us. This can be a challenge when caregivers ask about our families or want to get to know us more personally. Be gentle about how you handle these requests, and always think about the possible impact of what you will share, for yourself and for the relationship.

> Relationship building in a professional context means that you are friendly with the caregiver but not entering into a friendship.

Be mindful of physical barriers and body positioning. Whenever you can, minimize distractions that create a barrier between you and the caregiver. Many service coordinators and service providers take devices with them to type notes or get documents signed. Rather than opening your laptop or tablet and keeping it on your lap between you and the caregiver, leave it closed while you talk and only bring out the device when needed. Hiding behind your device, or even your thick folder of paperwork, makes relationship building harder because it can signal to the caregiver that you are more invested in the required activities of interviewing or document signing than in getting to know the person sharing the information or signing the form.

Other physical barriers can involve how you manage your own body in the family's space. Position yourself so that you are near the caregiver and child and ideally on the same level. Ask where the caregiver would like for you to sit or play. Dress professionally but appropriately for the work you do. Rather than feeling like you must protect your nice clothing, wear darker, washable fabrics so you can get messy. Do your best to be comfortable where the family is. Let the dog sit in your lap. Shrug off sticky toddler hands or baby drool on your shirt. Stash a change of clothes in your car in case you need to make a quick change between visits. (This served me well when I seemed to sit in a wet spot on the carpet on almost every visit with one potty-training family.)

Be responsive, collaborative, and reliable. Listen when the family expresses a need or asks a question and do your best to be responsive in a way that builds their capacity to get what they need for themselves. When problems arise, work together with the caregiver toward possible solutions (rather than trying to fix the problem for the family—more about this in Chapter 5). Relationships are built on trust so whenever you make a commitment to the family, whether it be agreeing to help find a resource or contacting the service coordinator to request an IFSP review, do what you say you would do. Always loop back to check in and make sure the issue has been addressed. Let them know you made the call or found the resource. Be a reliable partner.

Be respectful and compassionate, leaving your judgment at the door. You will meet families whose priorities, parenting styles, home environments, and interactions are vastly different from your own. Your values and beliefs about child rearing, cleanliness, and health may be challenged. No matter where you find yourself or with whom you interact, remember to always be respectful. You may not always like what someone does, but you can always show respect and compassion as a fellow human being. This involves being mindful about your body language, facial expressions, and the oral (or sign) language you use. I once heard a conference presenter who was a parent of a child with a disability say, "We know what you think of us, even when you don't say it. We know what you say about us when we aren't there." This was so memorable for me, not because I was thinking bad things about families, but because it reminded me about how our disposition toward families matters.

> You may not always like what someone does, but you can always
> show respect and compassion as a fellow human being. It is
> your job (not theirs) to meet the family where they are.

Being respectful also means leaving your judgment at the door and approaching each family with an objective point of view. You are a support to the family, and it is your job (not theirs) to meet them where they are. Look for common ground on which to build your partnership and when all else fails, remember that your mutual care for the child can ground you. Start there and approach each relationship with an open mind and heart. Embrace the belief that every parent is doing his or her best, and what that "best" looks like may differ from your own perspectives. None of us are perfect but all of us are trying. Suspend your judgment because it never serves the relationship. You never know, you might just learn something from a family who challenges your beliefs, so approach each relationship with compassion and respect—the same as you would want for yourself.

Pause

and REFLECT   What resonated with you about building reciprocal relationships with families? Capture 1–2 strategies or sentences here that you want to remember:

_____

_____

_____

_____

Skill 2: Prepare the Caregiver for Information Sharing

Similarly, taking the time to prepare the caregiver for the information gathering and sharing process conveys respect and partnership. Remember that for most families, entering into the EI system is a new experience. They often don't know what to expect or how things work. You can use the following strategies to help the caregiver understand what information is needed, why questions will be asked, and how that information will be used.

Focus on the specific step in the EI process for which information is necessary. During the initial visit or intake, it is typical to explain the big picture about how the EI process works, how we hope to work together, and what information we might need to gather to do that. Keep in mind that this initial explanation is not likely to be enough for a caregiver; you will need to revisit information sharing at each point in the EI process because the information required at each point might be different. Also, because EI is a new universe for many families, repeated explanations are likely to be helpful as the caregiver builds his or her knowledge base about the system. The EI process and the information gathered builds on itself as families move from that initial contact, through evaluation and assessment, on to IFSP development, and into service delivery. Because children and families are growing and changing, the information needed and what they share will also grow and change. Revisiting what information is needed, when, and why it is important, is an ongoing process.

Explain why you are asking. We often let families know that we will be asking questions about the child's activities, interests, preferences, strengths, and challenges. They probably expect that because they typically come to the system seeking help for their child. Caregivers might not expect that we will also ask about *their* (the caregiver's) interests, preferences, challenges, and thoughts about what they wish for the child and family. They also might be surprised when we dive deeper and inquire about family routines, activities, and resources. Whatever you are asking about, always explain why you are asking (hello, EI Adult Learning Principle 3). Remember that understanding *why* helps adult learners pay attention, share information, and become invested in the outcome of the information sharing. Helping families understand why something is important is an educational process as well; it gives them information they can use to make informed decisions, which is part of family-centered practice. Sharing the *why* also builds trust and mutual respect, which, as we have already seen, is essential for the EI relationship.

Describe how the information will be used. Right along with the *why* comes the *how*. EI programs usually have requirements for gaining permission to release information gathered from families that includes explanations about how the information will be used and documentation of family consent by parent signature. Privacy is important, and protecting the privacy of children and families is required by law under Part C of IDEA 2004 and reflected in guidance about parental rights and procedural safeguards. These are formal procedures that are often implemented with less formal conversations. You can use common language, avoiding technical jargon, and examples of how information will be used to help families understand. Explaining all of this may also make information sharing a little less uncomfortable. Or, if the caregiver is uncomfortable, further explanation should always include the caregiver's right to choose not to share. For example, including information about family concerns, priorities, and resources on the IFSP is voluntary. With further explanation (typically from the service coordinator) about how this information informs the rest of the IFSP and is useful for service delivery, most families will choose to include it. When you ask about the caregiver's goals for the child, explain that we want EI services to be grounded in what is most important to the family for the child's development. This helps us work together to write goals (i.e., IFSP outcomes) and determine services that are most appropriate to help the family work toward those goals. Helping families understand how information will be used also helps them connect the dots between their roles in the EI process and the decisions they can make, which is all part of building family capacity for active participation.

Partner with a language interpreter. For families who speak a language that is different from your own, a language interpreter is essential when helping prepare them to actively participate in the information gathering process. Not only are we required by law to provide information in a family's native language ("unless clearly not feasible to do so" per Part C of IDEA), the interpreter can help the family feel more comfortable with what is being asked and why. The interpreter can also help you adjust your style of information gathering so you are more mindful of cultural variables that might affect the process. The more you know, the more sensitive you can be while communicating with the family.

Emphasize the flexible nature of EI and the IFSP. When it is all said and done, remember that IFSP development is a fluid, flexible process. Information sharing will ebb and flow. Information will change as the child grows and the family's priorities, needs, and resources change. Any information included on the IFSP can be changed if needed—outcomes can be revised, services can be changed, and so on. Families can change their minds about consent for releasing information. They can decide to share more or less information at any time. Hopefully, though, if they feel well prepared for the information sharing process, they will be more comfortable having the conversations that make information sharing easiest.

Pause
and REFLECT
What resonated with you about preparing families for information sharing? Capture 1–2 strategies here that you want to remember:

_____

_____

_____

_____

Skill 3: Have a Reflective Conversation

Information sharing can sound like a formal process, especially when we think about documentation or look through the lens of an interview. I would suggest to you that gathering information from families does not have to be conducted via a formal interview. I know there are great tools out there to guide the conversation, and if you are comfortable with one of those tools, then by all means use it. Even in the context of an interview, however, I think you can use a less formal process of reflective conversation to gather deeper level information. With a reflective conversation, you and the caregiver (and the language interpreter if needed) can have a back-and-forth exchange of information and ideas. You can guide the conversation using the following strategies to help the caregiver share information that goes beyond typical interview questions and gets to the heart of how the child and family work and what they need.

Take a perspective of discovery. Maria Kastanis, a colleague with the Early Intervention Training Program at the University of Illinois, once shared this idea with me when talking about how service coordinators gather information from families. She suggested we approach information gathering from a "perspective of discovery." Think about that for a moment. When you first meet a family, there is so much you don't know and so much to discover. When you approach information gathering from a perspective of discovery, you drop your assumptions and remain open to receive whatever the caregiver chooses to share. You still guide the conversation with the questions you ask, but you don't assume you already know the answers. Instead, you remain curious. To do this, you must not only be mindful about how you ask questions and how you respond to the caregiver; you must also monitor your own thoughts and behaviors. When you feel judgment creep in, acknowledge it and let it go. When a negative thought pops up, breathe it out and replace it with two positives. We are only a very small part of families' stories; be open to discovering not only the part you will play but also the rest of the story as it unfolds.

> We are only a very small part of families' stories; be open to discovering not only the part you will play but also the rest of the story as it unfolds.

Weave open-ended questions and statements into the conversation. Discovery in the context of a reflective conversation reminds us to think about what we say and how we say it. Pay attention to how you invite caregivers to share information. Do you use lots of yes/no questions (like this one)? How do you use open-ended questions (like this) to learn about the child and family? Whenever you can, try to rephrase yes/no or close-ended questions to a more open-ended format that reflects that perspective of discovery. Try the exercise that follows for some practice.

Pause

to PRACTICE   *Instructions:* Review the list of questions below, and then revise them using an open-ended format. Open-ended questions typically look like *wh-* questions: *Who? What? When? Why? How?* Jot down a few of your favorite questions at the end, and if they are yes/no questions, try to rephrase them too. Turn to page 165 to compare your answers to mine.

Yes/no or Close-ended Questions	Open-ended Questions
Does your child say any words yet?	
Would you like to tell me about your day?	
Do you have any concerns?	
Can your baby sit up?	
Do you want the physical therapist to come to see you once a week?	
Jot down the questions you typically ask families here. Remember, try to phrase (or rephrase) them as open-ended questions.	

Reflective conversation requires a reciprocal exchange of ideas between you and the caregiver around a topic of importance or mutual interest. Sometimes, EI service providers say that reflecting with families can be challenging at first but gets easier as they get to know the family. Think of reflective conversation as a tool to use whenever you want to help the caregiver share information that explores the caregiver's prior knowledge and experience. Sound familiar? Reflective conversation is important when implementing EI Adult Learning Principle 2 because it allows you to learn about what caregivers think and what they know. It also explores what is most relevant to families (Principle 1) and sets the stage for the caregiver's active participation and practice with thinking about and sharing what they know (Principle 4). One of the things I love about reflective conversation is its capacity-building power. You are showing with your interest that you respect what the caregiver brings to the situation. Without a reflective conversation that helps the caregiver share thoughts, feelings, knowledge, and experience, you won't have the information you need to individualize the IFSP or the EI experience. With a better understanding of the caregiver's frame of reference, you will be more likely to develop an IFSP and provide services that match family needs and build on family strengths, so how you facilitate the conversation matters. Try the next activity to help you reflect on how different questions or statements you might use affect the type of information you gather from families.

Pause and REFLECT

Instructions: Match the question or statement with the information received from the family. Reflect on which questions or statements you use now and which you want to add to your repertoire (see Figure 4.3 on pages 93–97). Put a star beside any questions you think provide information that would be useful when writing IFSP outcomes. If you would like to check your matching with mine, turn to page 166.

Star	Question		Information Shared
	What time does Mason get up in the morning?		He loves spinning bowls on the kitchen floor and lining up his toy cars on the windowsill.
	What are Mason's favorite things to do?		He takes my hand and pulls me to the kitchen when he's thirsty or hungry. It's hard to figure out what he wants and we both get frustrated sometimes. I just have to keep showing him things in the fridge until I figure it out.
	Can Mason put any pieces in a puzzle yet?		8 a.m.
	How does Mason let you know when he wants something to eat or drink?		I wish we could play together, and he would talk like my other son. It's hard because he tantrums a lot during the day.
	What would you like to be able to do with Mason?		No, should he be able to?
	Does Mason eat a variety of foods?		Yes

Now, think about how you gather information from conversations with families. Note the questions and statements you frequently use below and whether they are open- or close-ended.

Question/Statement	Open?	Closed?	Revision
1. _____	❑	❑	_____
2. _____	❑	❑	_____
3 _____	❑	❑	_____

If any questions are closed, revise them using the open-ended format. Alternatively, review the list of questions that follows to see if you can find a revision. As you review, circle or highlight any questions you like. Make a list of these new questions and post them in your workspace so you can plan to use them on your next visit.

Open-ended Questions/Statements You Can Use to Facilitate Reflective Conversations:

◉ Tell me about your child's day.

◉ What would you like your child to be able to do?

◉ What would that look like to you (if your child could . . .)?

◉ How does your child communicate with you?

◉ How many words does your child say? What are some examples?

◉ What goes well with your child during the day?

◉ What times of day are challenging with your child? Why?

◉ What frustrates your child? What frustrates you?

◉ What do you and your child like to do together?

◉ What does your child like to do? What does your child not like to do?

◉ What would you like to be able to do with your child? As a family?

◉ If your child (or your family) could do _____, what would that look like to you?

◉ What have you already tried to help your child learn to _____?

◉ What would you be doing right now if I wasn't here?

◉ If this routine worked perfectly, what would that look like to you?

◉ What would make your life easier?

One more thing about using open-ended questions to facilitate reflective conversation: if you are partnering with an interpreter, be sure to explain to him or her how important the structure of the question is. This can be explained to the interpreter before the visit with the family. With an understanding of why open-ended questions are important, the interpreter will be more likely to successfully convey your questions as closely as possible to how you intended to ask them. This is important because our intention behind asking a reflective question can easily get lost in translation so be sure your interpreter understands how reflective conversation works too.

Look for opportunities for the caregiver to consider options, make decisions, and provide input. When you use open-ended questions and statements during a reflective conversation, you will often gather a great deal of information that informs how you support the family. You can listen for what goes well for the child and family, what is challenging, what they have already tried, what they want, and what is important to them. You may hear key points that you can use to help the family consider options and make decisions.

Let's think through an example. Imagine that you are chatting with Mel's family about their laundry routine. Mel is 18 months old and frequently pulls the laundry out of the basket while her mother tries to fold it. This was cute at first but now it has become a problem. This information was shared in the context of a discussion about daily routines that could potentially offer Mel learning opportunities for communication, movement, and sensory input. When you hear about the laundry routine, you think, "Oh, that sounds like a great opportunity for learning!" In this situation, it is important to be careful not to get carried away with what you think and instead check in with Mel's mother first, acknowledging her original concern. You might ask Mel's mother if she can show you what this routine looks like. Imagine that she brings out a basket of unfolded clothing and, as expected, Mel starts pulling clothes out and tossing them behind her. You could use your open-ended questions to ask, "What would this routine look like to you if it went well?" You could also ask if Mel's mother is interested in thinking about this routine as a learning opportunity, which could benefit Mel and distract her from the behavior that is problematic. You could provide a few examples, such as ideas for helping Mel learn to give each piece of clothing to her mother when asked, helping her learn to sort and label colors, prompting her to put the folded clothing back in the basket, and encouraging her to push the full basket into the bedroom when finished. You might see these activities as golden opportunities, but don't forgot that Mel's mother sees this routine as a problem. You can make space for Mel's mother to consider the option to explore this routine for possible learning opportunities and let her decide whether to use the ideas or discard them. She might want to try to engage Mel in the laundry routine, or she might want your help with ideas to stop Mel from interfering (such as thinking about options for folding the laundry on a surface that Mel cannot reach). It must be her choice. You can provide input without imposing your view of what she should do. Offering families opportunities to consider options and make decisions means you objectively provide information and input without ownership of the outcome. When you are tempted to push your own agenda (and let's be honest, we all have those moments) or are feeling frustrated when the caregiver makes a choice that you disagree with, remember who the outcome and who the intervention belongs to (hint: it's not you).

> Offering families opportunities to consider options and make decisions means you objectively provide information and input without ownership of the outcome.

Pause
and REFLECT
Which strategies for having reflective conversations resonated with you? Capture 1–2 strategies from this section that you want to remember:

_____

_____

_____

_____

Skill 4: Close the Communication Loop

The final skill in the information-gathering cycle involves closing the loop. Closing the communication loop includes summarizing what was just discussed or practiced, planning for what comes next, and then following through on any commitments you made.

Use the end of the reflective conversation to check in with the caregiver about his or her decision about which strategy to use or which action is needed. This could happen several times during a visit as you have conversations about the child's development or move in and out of problem solving, considering options, and identifying strategies the caregiver wants to try. Closing the loop might be the last thing that happens before you and the caregiver move into actively practicing strategies with the child during the visit or planning for how the strategies can be used between visits. When planning for what happens between visits, closing the communication loop could involve joint planning, which is one of the five characteristics of coaching described by Rush and Shelden (2020). Joint planning results from a conversation to determine what the caregiver wants to do between visits with the child, based on what was discussed and practiced during the visit. Joint planning also identifies what the caregiver wants to do at the next visit or what activities or routines will be addressed. We will discuss joint planning in more depth in Chapter 5.

> Closing the loop establishes you as a reliable partner who is paying attention and who is committed to the success of the child and family.

Finally, closing the loop involves you doing what you said you would do. If, for example, you made a commitment to contact the service coordinator to request an IFSP review, then do it and let the caregiver know you met your commitment with a quick follow-up call or text. If you promised to bring out a piece of therapy equipment to lend to the family, such as a wedge for the child who is learning to hold his head up while in prone, then don't forget to bring it to your next visit. Closing the loop establishes you as a reliable partner who is paying attention and who is committed to the success of the child and family. Strive to be the kind of partner each family needs.

Pause
and REFLECT   How can you make closing the loop an intentional process for you? Capture 1–2 strategies or sentences here that you want to remember:

_____

_____

_____

_____

Gathering meaningful information will always be easier in the context of a reciprocal, respectful relationship with the family that fosters open conversation and rich opportunities for caregivers to reflect, make decisions, receive support, and plan for next steps. What you learn from the family will inform what you do. Now that you are familiar with the information-sharing cycle, take a few moments to compare it to your own means of communicating with families. Notice what serves your relationship with families and what results in meaningful information gathering (and what does not). This activity has two parts: your own reflection and input from someone else. We can always try to assess ourselves accurately, but sometimes, especially with communication, inviting another person's perspective can really help us grow.

Pause and REFLECT

Instructions: Think of a recent interaction with a family during which you engaged in a conversation. Jot down how your interactions matched (or didn't match) the steps in the expanded information gathering cycle below (Figure 4.4). Note what you did, what information was shared, the outcome of the conversation, and how it had an impact on next steps. After your reflection, invite a colleague to observe a future visit. Ask this person to pay special attention to how you gather information. You can adapt the questions that follow to help your colleague provide constructive feedback, and then compare the notes to your own self-assessment and identify similarities and differences. Celebrate the strengths that bubble up, and intentionally plan for how you will address areas that need improvement. Be wide open to constructive feedback.

1. Briefly describe the context for the interaction with the family:

_____

_____

2. What information did you successfully gather?

_____

_____

3. Consider how you gathered information by reflecting on the cycle below.

_____

_____

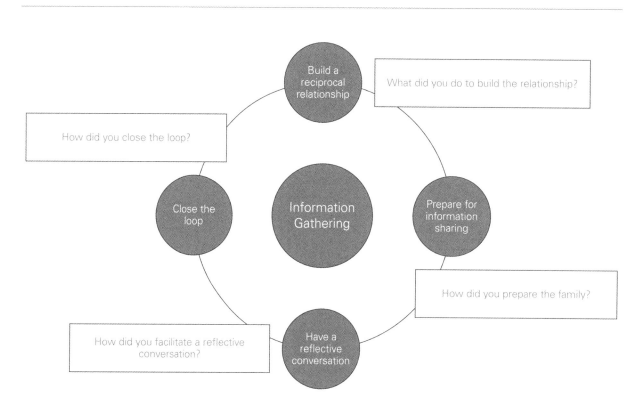

4. What information do you still need?

_____

_____

5. What information gathering skill(s) are you already using?

_____

_____

6. What skill(s) do you want to develop? What is your plan for improvement? (Hint: The more specific you are here, the more likely you will see change.)

_____

_____

GATHERING AND USING INFORMATION DURING INTAKE, EVALUATION AND ASSESSMENT, AND INDIVIDUALIZED FAMILY SERVICE PLAN DEVELOPMENT

Even before you have the chance to support a family during an intervention visit, there are important steps in the EI process during which information gathering is a necessity. The role you play in these initial steps will depend on how your program operates. If you are a service coordinator, you might begin learning about the child and family at the intake or initial visit. Or you might be a service provider who participates in the initial evaluation and assessment where you learn about the child's developmental skills, functional abilities, and how they affect and are affected by daily routines and interactions. Or, perhaps you participate in IFSP development, during which you use the information gathered to develop a meaningful plan for supports and services. Whether or not you participate in these initial steps that happen before the first intervention visit, you will definitely take part in ongoing assessment and IFSP review after you begin providing services to children and families. Let's think about how to use the information gathered during each of these important steps before we move to the next chapter, where we will dig into how to use what you learn to provide balanced intervention.

Intake

Although the information gathering process actually begins with the child's referral, the bulk of the earliest information is collected at the intake or initial visit. Typically, a service coordinator meets with the family to learn about their priorities, resources, and concerns for the child. Information is gathered about the child's medical history. Developmental, vision, and hearing screenings may be performed. Information is provided about the EI system and what to expect so that families can make informed decisions about their active participation. All of this information is later documented in the child's EI record. Here are a few tips for information gathering and sharing during the intake:

Attend to the relationship first. It can be tempting to jump right into more formal information gathering, especially if your program uses a true interview process. Instead, take time to chat with the family and begin to get to know the caregiver and child. Compliment the home, mention what a cute outfit the child is wearing, and/or ask about family pets. Use this time to break the ice and begin to build that reciprocal relationship. Have a friendly conversation with the caregiver and embed the questions you need to ask in it. I guarantee that you will learn meaningful insights about the child and family during this chat.

Observe while you chat. Pay attention to what the caregiver says while observing what he or she does with the child. Observe the child's interactions too. You can learn a lot about the child's development by simply watching what goes on in the background.

Encourage active participation and decision making from the beginning. Look for opportunities during the intake to lay the foundation for the caregiver's active participation. Provide information about the EI process and what to expect, and then encourage the caregiver to begin to think about preferences for the family. For example, you could begin planning for the initial evaluation and assessment during the intake by encouraging the caregiver to think about whom she wants to invite, such as a grandparent, or perhaps she really wants to be sure a speech-language pathologist is present. You could emphasize the importance of sharing information with the professionals on the assessment team to help them understand a challenging routine or activity. The caregiver could decide how to share this information, such as by recording a short video to show or jotting down notes about what happens during daily life. In looking for these opportunities, you are helping caregivers begin to understand the value of their role in their child's intervention.

Look for opportunities during the intake to lay the foundation for the caregiver's active participation and help the caregiver think about preferences for the family.

Initial Evaluation and Assessment

After the intake visit, the next big step for families involves the evaluation and assessment. These are often thought of as one combined step but really they are two separate activities. The evaluation involves gathering information about the child and using it to determine eligibility for EI services. The assessment is a more extensive information gathering process during which we learn details about a child's development and the family's priorities, daily routines, and activities that are needed to write (and later review) the IFSP. We often think of evaluation and assessment as activities during which we test children using toys and tools. Team members convene at the family's home or in the office. We play with the child, often using toys the child has never seen, while asking the parent lots of questions about what the child does and does not do. We gather functional information by asking about and observing how the child participates in natural family activities and listening for what goes well and what is a struggle. We use what we learn to score our tests and determine a number (age-equivalent or standardized score) that helps us decide if the child is eligible for services. We share the results of the evaluation and assessment with the family and then, with parental permission, move to the next step and begin developing the IFSP. Yes, evaluation and assessment are important opportunities for us to gather information, but we also need to remember they can be life-changing events in families' lives. How we gather information, how we observe and ask questions, how we engage the parent and the child—all of that matters not only with how effective our information gathering is but also with how comfortable the process is for the family.

Here's an important takeaway from this section: Evaluation and assessment are so much more than marking checks and minuses on a test or watching to see if a child can stack blocks. They are doorways into and paths through EI services. Gathering specific, meaningful information at this point in the process defines where we begin with service delivery and requires particular skills to make sure what you learn matches what you need to know. These skills will continue to be needed throughout the EI process as you conduct ongoing assessment to monitor the child's progress too. Let's pause and reflect on how you gather information, and then I will share some dos and don'ts based on the following self-assessment.

> Gathering specific, meaningful information at this point in the process defines where we begin with service delivery and requires particular skills to make sure what you learn matches what you need to know.

Pause
and REFLECT

Instructions: Complete this brief self-assessment to reflect on the skills you use to gather developmental information at the initial evaluation and assessment.

Self-Assessment: Gathering Information From Families About Development

Item	Never	Not Very Often	Sometimes	Most of the Time	Always	Notes to Explain My Answers
I ask mostly open-ended questions to gather information about the child's development.						
I have conversations with families about development.						
I situate developmental questions in the context of everyday activities.						
I gather information by observing the child's development while he or she plays and interacts with others.						
I explain what I am looking for before or while observing.						

(continued)

Item	Never	Not Very Often	Sometimes	Most of the Time	Always	Notes to Explain My Answers
I explain why I am gathering information or trying an activity with the child.						
I actively listen to the family to learn what is important to them.						
I involve the caregiver in engaging the child to help me gather information (i.e., ask the caregiver to try an activity with the child while I observe).						
I recognize the value of gathering functional information about the child's everyday life versus focusing solely on the items on my developmental checklist.						
I invite the caregiver to ask questions frequently throughout our conversation rather than preferring to wait until later to answer them.						

Next, review your answers and place a star beside any skill that you want to improve or develop further, and then note how you will do that over the next month or two.

_____

_____

Finally, select a specific item from the self-assessment and plan your next steps.

To improve my skills with _____, I will:

❐ Approach my next five conversations with families about child development mindfully with the goal of practicing an improvement in this skill

❐ Take time to observe a colleague who has this skill well developed

❏ Record myself on video with a family so I can reflect and learn from it

❏ Ask a colleague to observe me (or my video) and provide feedback

❏ Discuss my skills with my supervisor or a colleague and invite suggestions and feedback

❏ Read an article or watch a video about the skill and implement a tip I learn

❏ Jot down notes after each of my next five conversations with families about child development to reflect on what I did well and what still needs improvement

To help you think more deeply about gathering developmental information, here are some dos and don'ts based on the self-assessment you just completed (see Figure 4.2). Be honest with yourself about where your practices fall between the dos and don'ts, and look for opportunities where you can grow.

DO use open-ended questions whenever you can. Ex: *How does Josie communicate with you? What does she do to let you know what she wants or needs?*	DON'T use yes/no questions for the majority of your information gathering. Ex: *Does Josie use words yet?*
Tip: Remember, open-ended questions allow the caregiver to decide how to answer and what to share. They also invite interpretation, which opens the door for information that is specific to the child's and family's experience. Yes/no questions limit the level of detail you receive. You will inevitably have to ask yes/no questions, but whenever you can rephrase and use an open-ended question, go that route.	
DO ask about development in the context of a friendly conversation. Ex: *So, what kinds of things does Josie like to eat? When she eats her cucumber slices, how does she feed herself?*	DON'T grill the caregiver in a rapid-fire interview-style question-and-answer session. Ex: *Does Josie use her fingers to self-feed? Does she pinch food between her thumb and forefinger? Can she get the food from her tray to her mouth?*
Tip: Interview questions are helpful, especially when you are first learning how to gather information. Review and memorize what you need to know so you can gather the same information in the context of a friendly conversation, which is more likely to put the caregiver at ease.	
DO situate your developmental questions in the context of the child's and family's everyday activities. Ex: *What does Josie like to do when she plays outside?*	DON'T ask too many generic questions out of context. Ex: *Can Josie walk on uneven surfaces?*
Tip: Listen and learn about the family's daily activities and preferences. Tap into them to learn about the child's development. For instance, when a caregiver mentions bath time, follow that path and ask about what bath time looks like, what the child does, what the caregiver does, what goes well, what's challenging, etc. You can learn a lot about cognition, communication, adaptive, social, and motor development by exploring a routine like bath time. You might also get a sense of cultural- and family-specific expectations for development and child participation by exploring a specific routine, which are important things to know as you interpret assessment information.	

FIGURE 4.2.   Dos and don'ts for information gathering.

DO observe the child's development and explain what you are looking for. Ex: *I'd like to watch how Josie moves around by herself, if that's okay. I'm looking to see how she uses her balance and coordinates her movements.*	**DON'T** observe the child's development and take notes or comment on what she cannot yet do without explanation. Ex: *I see she's not yet climbing up the stairs . . .* (checking an item on the test).

Tip: Ask for permission to observe and always explain why. When you see the child doing something that informs you about development, talk about it with the caregiver and be sensitive and kind. If you take any notes, explain what you are writing and offer the caregiver the opportunity to review what you wrote.

DO explain to the caregiver what you are doing and why you are trying to get the child to do an activity. Ex: *I'm going to see how Josie can stack these cubes after she sees me doing it. This helps me understand how she uses her eye–hand coordination, her attention, and her problem-solving skills. It also helps me understand if she can imitate what she sees me do.*	**DON'T** engage the child in an activity without explaining to the caregiver what you are doing and why. Ex: *Josie, can you stack these cubes like this?* You try to get Josie to stack 1-inch cubes and when she cannot, you make a note without explaining to the caregiver what you are looking for and why it matters.

Tip: If information gathering involves engaging the child in play activities (such as during a developmental screening or assessment), narrate what you are doing. Explain how the activity helps you learn about development. If the child is not successful with the activity, explain what you saw and what that might mean, relating the activity to the child's abilities and struggles in everyday life.

DO actively listen to gather information about what is important to the family, what is most relevant, and what they need. Ex: You let the caregiver know you are interested and you value what she is saying using your body language and active listening skills. You also listen for and comment on the priorities and needs shared by the caregiver, which will be integrated into the IFSP and addressed during service delivery.	**DON'T** listen for only the information you think you need, such as the answers to your interview checklist. Ex: You pay more attention to your checklist than you do to what the caregiver is sharing.

Tip: Lean toward the caregiver, nod your head, and use your voice to convey interest. Listen for more than developmental milestones. Listen for information about concerns, priorities, resources, daily activities, interests, and family routines. Note what goes well, what frustrates the caregiver and/or child, what they enjoy, what they would like to be able to do, and what is important to their family. All of this is just as important as whether the child can put shapes in a three-piece puzzle.

DO involve the caregiver in engaging the child during the information-gathering process. Ex: *Josie might be more comfortable with you reading the book with her because she doesn't know me. Would you mind trying? I'd like to see if she can point to any pictures you name for her.*	**DON'T** discourage the caregiver from engaging with the child during the information-gathering process. Ex: *I need to see if Josie will point to pictures without any help when I name them.*

Tip: Ask if the caregiver can show you what the child typically does. Invite the caregiver to interact with the child in a new way so you can see what happens (while always explaining why). Having someone watching may feel uncomfortable for the caregiver at first (and maybe for you too) but this contributes to that foundation of active caregiver participation and can provide you with information you may not have learned by just asking about development or trying to engage the child yourself.

FIGURE 4.2. *(continued)*

DO pay attention to functional information and what it tells you about the child's development. Ex: *What does Josie do when she wants something but can't communicate it clearly?* Her mother describes how, when Josie wants something to drink and can't reach her cup, she will push a chair over to the counter and climb up to try to get what wants. This tells you a lot about Josie's abilities to problem-solve and get her needs met.	DON'T ignore functional information because it does not exactly match with the question you ask or the item you are trying to score on your assessment. Ex: When her mother shares the example, you redirect her by saying: *That's great, but what sounds does Josie make?*

Tip: There is specific information you will need to gather to complete your screening or assessment tool, and that is important. Information about how the child participates in everyday activities (or doesn't) that might not be reflected on a tool is important too. Be open to both kinds of information because without both, your job to meet the mission of early intervention will be harder.

DO invite the caregiver to ask questions. Ex: *What questions can I answer about the screening today?*	DON'T tell the caregiver to not interrupt or hold her questions until later. Ex: *I can answer that question when I'm finished with our interview.*

Tip: Remember your partnership and the reciprocal exchange of information that is part of gathering information. Pause frequently for questions and do your best to answer them honestly. When you don't know, say so but do your best to find the answer and follow up.

Pause

to PLAN   Whew, that was a lot to take in. Pause now to jot down at least one idea from the dos and don'ts that you want to remember and how will you implement that idea during your next evaluation or assessment.

_____

_____

_____

A note about functional assessment. Conducting the initial evaluation and assessment can be a complex task because so much information gathering is required in a space where you hardly know the family. It can be easy to lean heavily on your assessment tool because that is what you are familiar with—it is the *known* for you. Consider this: knowing what a child can or cannot do according to a formal test is only useful because it provides us with a standard against which to compare development. We know how the child performs tasks compared to other children or compared to himself (eventually across time). What is likely missing from most of our tools is the connection between the skills the child performed (or didn't) and their impact on the child's and family's daily life. That is where gathering functional information becomes so important. If a child cannot stack 1-inch cubes, so what? Perhaps he struggles with this because he does not yet have the ability to sustain his attention (at an age-appropriate level) or imitate what others do. Maybe motor planning is hard for him. What is important here is that a child who struggles with attention or imitation might also have trouble with social interaction or with learning from others, which affects many other abilities. If motor planning is the real challenge, then his performance with the blocks (and probably other tasks like putting pegs in a bottle or imitating strokes with a crayon) could help you and his family understand why he throws his toys constantly and struggles to use a spoon to feed himself. Development is naturally complex. Out of context, the skills on an assessment tool don't really help you understand this complexity. Gathering functional information provides you with the context you need to translate the complexity of test items into individualized information about each child and family. This allows you, as part of the IFSP team, to better understand their strengths and challenges and write outcomes with the family that will be meaningful in their everyday life. Stacking blocks or putting pegs in a bottle are not functional outcomes. Being able to purposefully take turns rolling a ball back and forth, pretend with a kitchen set during family time after dinner, or coordinate a spoon to feed oneself gooey macaroni and cheese—these are functional skills that matter to families and are what we need to focus on during assessment and IFSP development.

Gathering functional information provides you with the context you need to translate the complexity of test items into individualized information about each child and family.

Individualized Family Service Plan Development

Developing the IFSP is where all of the rich information you have gathered about a child and family comes together into a plan for EI service delivery. Remember that the *I* in IFSP stands for *individualized*. If this information does not help us understand what is unique about the family's priorities, daily routines and interactions, and the child's specific developmental strengths and needs, then the plan will likely lack the *I*. For EI practitioners like you and me, it can be really easy to meet a toddler, listen to a family, and think we know what is going on or what is needed based on our clinical experience. Sure, we went to school for years and have worked hard in the field to develop our expertise. No matter how knowledgeable or experienced you are, however, you can never know precisely how to apply your knowledge or experience without learning what is unique about and meaningful to the family.

No matter how knowledgeable or experienced you are, you can never know precisely how to apply your knowledge or experience without learning what is unique about and meaningful to the family.

At its core, IFSP development is the process during which all of the information we gather at intake, evaluation, and assessment is used to connect the dots between what families know and want for their children, what children do and need to learn, and what we understand about intervention and family support. It is also a time when we share a great deal of information to facilitate the family's participation in the development of the plan. The dots we connect between what we know and what the family knows, and the picture they make, will look different for each child and family. Summary information from the intake and assessment, which is included in the IFSP, helps us understand the child's development in the context of daily routines and activities—if we translate that information from test skills and scores to impact on child and family life. Outcome (or goal) development takes this translation further as we collaborate with families to link their priorities for their children with the next steps the child needs to take for developmental progress. Services are then determined based on the outcomes included in the plan when the team (including the family) asks themselves, "Who is the most appropriate service provider to assist this family with working toward the outcomes that are important to them?" Decisions about outcomes, services, and even the child's future transition out of EI (which is always discussed at IFSP meetings) are based on the information we gather—and what we share—so it is especially important to take time to reflect on just how to gather and share that important information.

As you did with the evaluation and assessment section, pause now to complete a quick self-assessment, then consider dos and don'ts when reflecting on your own IFSP development practices.

Pause

and REFLECT
Instructions: The self-assessment below will help you think about how you gather, share, and use information to develop meaningful IFSPs. Keep in mind that the information you gather to write the IFSP affects the services provided (either by you or another practitioner).

Self-Assessment: Gathering, Sharing, and Using Information for IFSP Development

Item	Never	Not Very Often	Sometimes	Most of the Time	Always	Notes to Explain My Answers
I have conversations with families about how they would like to participate in IFSP development.						
I translate assessment results for families to help them understand the connections between test skills and what they see with their child's strengths and needs in their daily life.						
I focus on functional activities rather than test skills when discussing IFSP outcomes.						
I situate the discussion about outcomes in the context of everyday activities.						
I access the expertise of all team members (including the family) when discussing outcomes and learning opportunities.						

(continued)

Item	Never	Not Very Often	Sometimes	Most of the Time	Always	Notes to Explain My Answers
I ask mostly open-ended questions to gather information about the family's priorities for the child's development to prepare for writing outcomes.						
I pause and check in with caregivers to answer questions and gain input.						
I help write outcomes that are based on what is important to the family (rather than what is important to me).						
I use input from the family to determine how to make outcomes measurable.						
I invite families to participate in the discussion about service options and identify what they think would work best for them.						
I participate in transition planning that helps families understand their options and make informed decisions.						

As you did before, review your answers and place a star beside any skill you want to improve or develop further, and then note how you will do that the next time you participate in an IFSP meeting.

_____

_____

Finally, select a specific item from the self-assessment and plan your next steps.

To improve my skills with _____, I will:

❐ Approach my next five conversations with families about child development or the IFSP mindfully with the goal of practicing an improvement in this skill

❐ Take time to observe a colleague who has this skill well developed

❐ Record myself on video with a family so I can reflect and learn from it

☐ Ask a colleague to observe me (or my video) and provide feedback

☐ Discuss my skills with my supervisor or a colleague and invite suggestions and feedback

☐ Read an article or watch a video about the skill and implement a tip I learn

☐ Jot down notes after each of my next five conversations with families about child development or the IFSP to reflect on what I did well and what still needs improvement

> To help you think more deeply about your practices related to IFSP development, here are some dos and don'ts based on the self-assessment you just completed. Again, be honest with yourself as you reflect and embrace the places where you see opportunities for your own professional development.

DO explain the individualized family service plan (IFSP) development process so families know what to expect and can decide how they would like to participate.	DON'T just tell families what will happen to them or what to do.
Ex: *If your child is eligible for early intervention (EI), you will have the opportunity to develop an individualized family service plan, or IFSP. During this process, we'll talk about your goals for your child's development and how to help you help him work toward them. We'll also talk about what service you and your child might receive. We'll talk about options and you'll be an important part of these decisions. We really value your thoughts and opinions during this process. Feel free to jot down notes about what you want before we meet or you can even send me a video to show any activities your child does well or struggles with. You can also invite anyone you want to the IFSP meeting.*	Ex: *We will develop an IFSP after your child is found eligible. This is the service plan that outlines the outcomes and services your child will receive. The team will decide what to work on based on the assessment and what service is most appropriate to address your child's needs. By the end of the IFSP meeting, you will know what service your child will receive.* (Yikes, this is not at all family centered!)

Tip: Hopefully, the IFSP development process will be explained to the family during the intake or initial visit. It is still a good idea to briefly reexplain the process after the assessment and before the family consents to write an IFSP. Be sure to explain the IFSP acronym at this point (and periodically in the future because it takes time for families to learn the lingo). Look for opportunities for the family to actively participate in the process by considering decisions, planning for participation, asking questions, and sharing their ideas or information about their daily life. Be specific about these decision points and pause for the caregiver to think and make decisions. It's a lofty process so give the caregiver the space needed to learn, consider, and decide what's best for the family.

Here's something else to consider. Whenever we talk about "the team" to a family, as we see here in our "Don't" example, we separate the family from the rest of the team. Reflect on the words you use to explain the assessment and IFSP development processes and make sure that anytime you use the word "team," you include the caregiver, without whom there would be no team.

FIGURE 4.3. Dos and don'ts for individualized family service plan development.

DO help families understand the connections between test skills and their child's strengths and struggles by explaining the underlying abilities that test skills demonstrate when summarizing assessment results in the body of the IFSP.	DON'T list the test items the child can or cannot do on the IFSP without providing context or linking them to daily life.
Example from the assessment summary on Adam's IFSP: "Adam seems to love his cat and will look for her when his mom asks, 'Where's Pickles?' He is not yet using words to communicate but he does make some vowel sounds and has said 'dada' several times. In general, he does not yet seem to be paying attention to what others say or trying to imitate what he hears, which limits his opportunities to learn what words mean and how to imitate sounds and words to communicate what he wants. Some of Adam's strengths seem to be how he uses his hands and his independent problem-solving skills, which we see when he scribbles and draws on apps on the family's iPad, puts floor puzzles together on his own, and pulls a chair over to the counter to climb up and get cookies, which he can feed himself using his fingers. He is not yet taking turns or imitating others, which we noticed when we tried to get him to imitate stacking blocks or take turns rolling a ball back and forth. He prefers to play on his own according to his mom. Adam's independence is a strength for him but his struggles with social interaction and communication seem to interfere with his ability to learn from others. Helping him learn to engage, take turns, imitate playful activities, and use sounds or early words to communicate what he wants or needs will be important next steps for his development."	Example from the assessment summary on Adam's IFSP: "Adam was able to scribble in an iPad, pick up a small object using a pincer grasp, and use a chair to climb up on the counter. He was not able to stack blocks, imitate strokes, or take turns with another person. He spontaneously makes vowel sounds and has said 'dada' several times per parent report. He is not yet understanding simple directions but will look for the cat when he hears her name."

Tip: When summarizing your assessment observations, it is always a good idea to balance a strengths-based approach with an honest appraisal of the child's needs. Rather than listing the assessment skills the child could and could not do, relate strengths and challenges to your observations and what the caregiver described about everyday life. Help the caregiver understand the underlying abilities that test skills demonstrate and how they help us understand why something may or may not be occurring in the child's development. This understanding can also help the caregiver learn why a child behaves in a certain way, why he struggles with a certain routine, and what we can do to help him learn new skills or improve the routine. Rather than focusing on the test skills, mention them and then explain what they tell us about the child's development—be intentional about making this connection for the family (and for other team members). To do this, you have to make sure you have a thorough understanding of why a test item is important and what underlying abilities the specific task demonstrates. If this is a new idea for you, take some time and dissect items on the test you use. Think about what each item tells you about different areas of development and consider underlying abilities and processing, such as executive function, sensory integration, quality of movement, etc.

FIGURE 4.3. *(continued)*

DO combine what you learned about the child's development from the assessment with what the family shares about their priorities and the child's functional strengths and needs when developing IFSP outcomes.

Example from IFSP discussion: "Ava exhibited delays in gross motor development during her assessment, which her grandmother expected. Ava pulls herself forward on her belly but is not yet getting on hands and knees in preparation for crawling. She can sit by herself when placed in sitting but struggles with transitions in and out of sitting." After discussing this with her grandmother, who described their regular play time each morning after she gets Ava dressed, Ava's IFSP outcomes read: "1) Ava will get to her hands and knees and crawl five steps forward to get to her grandmother when she calls her name or shakes Ava's stuffed bunny during four morning playtimes in a row; and 2) Ava will transition from sitting to crawling and back again at least three times during each morning playtime with her grandmother over 1 week."

DON'T pick IFSP outcomes directly from missing test items or write outcomes for families using a clinical perspective.

Example from IFSP discussion: "Based on assessment results, the physical therapist recommended the following IFSP outcomes: 1) Ava will assume a hands and knees position to crawl forward three feet without assistance; and 2) Ava will transition between sitting and all fours 3 out of 5 attempts during each visit."

Tip: You probably noticed that integrating the family priorities and routines into an IFSP outcome made for a longer outcome statement. That's okay and encouraged. Here's why. When the outcome includes the family's language and reflects their routines, activities, and interests, they are more likely to identify with it, own it, and remember what to do to address it. If, on the other hand, the outcomes sound clinical or read like the professional must be present to work on them or measure progress, the caregiver may be less likely to embrace his or her active role in encouraging the child's development. I truly believe that words matter. It takes practice to learn to individualize outcome statements, so if this is new to you, here's a tip for sharpening your skills. Make a list of outcomes you've helped write recently or outcomes you've seen on IFSPs. Take what you know about the child and revise the statement to integrate the child's interests, family interactions, and specific routines. Compare the two and think about which one the family will be more likely to identify with. Then, take this experience and use what you learn during real IFSP meetings. You'll be amazed at the difference in family involvement.

DO invite family members to share their goals first, based on what they want for the child and what they learned from the assessment, and then encourage other team members to use their expertise to support a family-centered outcome development process.

Ex: When it is time to develop the IFSP and discuss outcomes, Leslie, service coordinator and developmental therapist, turns to Ben's father first to discuss his priorities. She asks, "At the intake, we talked about Ben's tantrums and his frustration about not being able to talk. Based on the assessment and what's important to you about Ben's development, what would you like Ben to be able to do in the next six months to a year?" When Ben's father says that he would like his son to talk in sentences, she invites the speech-language pathologist (SLP) to join the conversation to brainstorm ideas for outcomes and strategies. All three team members (Ben's father, Leslie, and the SLP) then discuss family routines when communication is important and strategies, such as using simple sign language as a temporary communication bridge, that might help Ben. Ben's father is an important and equal part of the discussion.

DON'T turn to professional team members to write IFSP outcomes while family team members sit passively by.

Ex: When it is time to develop the IFSP and discuss outcomes, Leslie turns to the SLP and asks her, "What do you think Ben's outcome should be?" The SLP explains that Ben should be saying well over 100–200 words at his age so using sign language might be a good idea to help him communicate. Leslie and the SLP write outcomes for Ben to be able to use sign language and simple words to label and request objects. Ben's father quietly listens and wonders, because they are talking about sign language, if they think Ben will never learn to talk.

Tip: Professional team members bring their valued expertise, knowledge, and skills with intervention to the IFSP meeting. Their input is always welcome, but so is the input of the caregiver who brings expertise about the child's and family's daily life. The IFSP outcome discussion requires a balance that integrates the expertise of all team members. Even though you may feel strongly that a particular skill or developmental area should be addressed when outcomes are written, take a moment to hang back and let the caregiver share first. Often, there will be overlap between the caregiver's priorities and what you think because you are working together to understand the child's development. When family goals and your goals are different, try not to push your opinion to force an outcome on the plan. Instead, share what you know and then let the caregiver decide if now is the time to address it. If not, then trust in the service coordinator (and future service provider, if not you) to address all important aspects of the child's development later. Sometimes, starting with what is most important to the family can be hard, but with time to build trust and a strong relationship, team members are able to help families understand the child's development in new ways and doors open to strategies that might not have made sense early on. Trust the process and remember that the IFSP belongs to the family, not to you.

DO ask open-ended questions to learn about family priorities, what they want to see their children be able to do, and what they need. Ex: *What would you like to see your child doing in the next 6 months or in a year? When you think about Abby talking, what would you like her to say? What would it look like to you if Kairo was able to move about by himself? How can we help you help Liam?*	**DON'T use close-ended questions or statement that assume you know what outcomes should be included or what services the child should receive.** Ex: *Do you want to Abby to use two-word phrases in the next 6 months? How about we write a goal for Kairo to walk 20 feet using his gait trainer? Liam should be interacting more with others so he needs weekly special instruction. Does that sound good to you?*

Tip: You do have valuable information to share during the IFSP development process. Yes, you will provide guidance and share your expertise. Whenever you can, however, gather information from the family first to find out what they know, what they understand, and what they need. Be careful to avoid assuming you know because you have worked with so many families or because you have expertise in a certain area. Keep this in mind when discussing the outcomes and service options because family input is essential to both.

DO ask the caregiver what the outcome would look like when it was met and use this information to measure success. Ex: When asked about how to measure Eleanor's success with learning to walk and what this would look like for the family, her mother says she would be so happy if Eleanor could walk from the door of the mall to the play area on her own. That way, her mother would not have to carry Eleanor while pushing her infant brother's stroller. With this information, the team writes this outcome: "Eleanor will walk 20 feet from the door to the play area independently each week for a month when her family visits the mall." This outcome describes how progress will be measured by all team members. When Eleanor can walk to the play area consistently, it will be time to celebrate!	**DON'T skip measurability or tack on generic criteria like "throughout the day."** Ex: When asked what outcome should be included on Eleanor's IFSP, the physical therapist checks his assessment tool and notes that Eleanor is not yet taking more than a few steps without falling down. He suggests the following outcome: "Eleanor will walk independently without falling down throughout the day." This outcome is very similar to the generic outcomes on other IFSPs of toddlers with motor delays in this program and fails to include the context during which progress will be measured so that all team members understand the goal.

Tip: Part C of IDEA 2004 requires that outcomes must be measurable, but how the criteria for measurement are determined and how rigorous these criteria are vary across programs and states. A good rule is to include criteria that are grounded in family activities and specific enough so that all team members can recognize the end goal or when the family will feel that the outcome is met. A very specific, measurable outcome (like Eleanor's mall play area outcome) does not mean that therapy only takes place during the one activity included in the outcome. Instead, for Eleanor, all team members will know that the outcome is met when Eleanor's mother says her daughter independently walks to the play area on multiple trips to the mall. When Eleanor can do this, she will most likely be walking in other situations too, so we can be assured that she's mastered this ability.

FIGURE 4.3. *(continued)*

DO facilitate a team discussion about service delivery options and recommendations that offers families opportunities to make choices and consider what would best meet their needs.

Ex: *Based on the outcome we just wrote to help Sydney learn to safely bottle feed with less spillage so she can gain weight, we have some options for services. The occupational therapist has expertise in feeding, so she could be a good match to help with this goal. How often do you think you would like support? The OT can come out 2×/week at first and then back down to weekly or every other week as you feel confident that Sydney is making progress. Or she can come out weekly if you feel like 2×/week would be more than you need. Visits range from 30 to 60 minutes. How long do you feel like you would like the visits to last?*

DON'T prescribe services, frequency or length of visits, or location based on the child's delay or disability, your own schedule, or "what most children receive."

Ex: *The occupational therapist has space on her caseload for a weekly visit, so that's what we recommend. She typically sees infants for 30-minute visits to address feeding, so that's what you can expect. Does this sound okay to you?*

Tip: Logistics about service delivery can be tricky to determine, especially when factors such as provider shortages, travel distance, and billing requirements come into play. Always do your best to individualize the service determination discussion and offer options with lots of information to help the caregiver decide what is best for the family. It is very common for family members to feel unsure of how much service they need, and that is okay. Just don't take their uncertainty as an invitation to tell them what they need. Try your best to consider what you know about the family and offer options when there are options to consider. There is no research evidence that tells us that all children need weekly services, although that is the most common frequency we see in EI (IDEA Infant Toddler Coordinators Association, 2019). Consider factors such as how often you expect the child's needs to change, how much support the parent might need initially, and how complex the child and family needs are when determining service frequency (Jung, 2003). Remember, too, that service type, frequency, and length can always be adjusted. Be sure families know this too.

DO help families understand and prepare for the transition process by discussing community options so they can make decisions about what's best for them.

Ex: At Dustin's initial IFSP meeting, Jada describes what transition means and makes sure that his parents understand future timelines and options to consider. She revisits transition frequently at IFSP review meetings and, as Dustin gets closer to his third birthday, she focuses more on transition planning so that his parents can consider options in their community. Because Dustin still shows some delays due to his cerebral palsy, Jada shares information about the early childhood special education (ECSE) preschool program at their local elementary school but invites them to learn about other options, too, such as private therapy, other preschools, and so forth. The transition discussion continues so that when the time comes for Dustin to leave the EI program, he and his family are ready for their next steps.

DON'T assume all children are going to transition to the same destination, such as ECSE.

Ex: At Dustin's initial IFSP and subsequent reviews, Jada frequently mentions the ECSE preschool program as the best option for Dustin's future transition after EI. As Dustin gets closer to age 3, his parents are more interested in his neighborhood preschool where he can learn with his friends. Jada tells them they can certainly consider that as an option but because Dustin has cerebral palsy, the ECSE preschool is probably more appropriate for his needs because more of the children in EI transition there.

Tip: Different communities will have different options, some having more or fewer than others. The service coordinator is the EI team member who coordinates the transition process, which should be another opportunity for the family to be active participants and decision makers. It is important to help families consider whatever options are available and then respect their choices. If you are not a service coordinator, it is still important for you to be aware of community options and what toddlers need as they prepare to receive support after EI, if their families so choose. Just remember that transition is a milestone in many families' lives. It can be a scary process to move from EI, where families have lots of support, to center-based settings where the child is away from the parent and services become more child focused. It can also be a time to celebrate the child's progress. Be mindful that this experience can be equally hard and wonderful for families and provide emotional and informational support as families move into the next phase of their child's development and education.

Pause
to PLAN

Instructions: Write down at least one tip you want to remember to use during IFSP development and how will you use this tip during your next IFSP meeting.

_____

_____

_____

_____

EMBRACING THE LINK
BETWEEN INFORMATION AND INTERVENTION

Knowing how to gather and share meaningful information with families throughout the EI process are key skills for all practitioners. You might think this is most important for service coordinators, but I would challenge you to think about how much easier your job is as a therapist or educator when you know the family well. Paying attention to what parents and other caregivers say (and how they say it), asking open-ended questions to help them share what's important, and relating what you learn to what you know about child development and intervention are things you probably do without even thinking. If, however, while reading this chapter you came across a new idea or discovered something you do that you would like to change, make a commitment to yourself to embrace what you learned.

Your efforts to learn with and about families will directly affect the support you provide. All of the valuable information you learn from the intake, evaluation and assessment, and IFSP development processes prepare you for how best to collaborate with caregivers for successful intervention, whether you are the person who actually gathers this information or not. With that said, there will be much more to learn as you get to know the family in the trenches of regular intervention visits. This kind of in-depth information takes time to gather as you visit the family, join their activities and routines, learn what makes them tick, and come to hopefully understand how to support them so they feel confident encouraging their child's development every day. This will likely be easier with some families than others, but when you enter the relationship from a perspective of discovery, with a deep respect for the love the family has for the child and the knowledge they bring to the table, you will be in a better position to share what you know during service delivery in a way that builds on family strengths and empowers family confidence. Every step in the EI process, as in child development, builds on the next. It is time for the next step, no, giant *leap* into EI service delivery.

"

ALL KNOWLEDGE IS
CONNECTED TO ALL
OTHER KNOWLEDGE.
THE FUN IS IN MAKING
THE CONNECTIONS.

"

—Arthur C. Aufderheide

CHAPTER 4

Reflective Journal

Instructions: Use this space to capture your thoughts about what you learned in Chapter 4.

NEW IDEAS: _____

_____

_____

_____

_____

_____

IDEAS THAT CHALLENGED ME: _____

_____

_____

_____

_____

_____

THOUGHTS & FEELINGS: _____

_____

_____

_____

_____

_____

Action Plan

Instructions: Based on your reflections in this chapter, what do you want to do next? Be sure to check in with yourself periodically to see if you are following the intention you set here. If not, review the chapter and make a new plan. You are in charge of what you do.

By _____ (date),

I will take responsibility for how I intentionally gather information from families by _____

_____ (action).

(actions examples: asking open-ended questions to learn more about family priorities, gathering more functional information at the assessment, including child and family activities as context for IFSP outcomes)

ACTION PLAN COMPLETED ☐

My key takeaway: _____

_____

_____

TIPS:

- After your next intake or assessment, block 20 minutes to reflect on the information you gathered and how you gathered it. Ask yourself what you did that matches what you learned in this chapter. If you find opportunities for improvement, write them down and keep them handy for when you schedule your next intake or assessment so you can go to the meeting prepared to be mindful about what you want to do.

- Invite your colleagues to get together for lunch to chat about how they gather information from families and use it to write the IFSP. Share the self-assessments in this chapter with the group and ask them to complete the self-assessments before the meeting. Invite each colleague to share insights learned, and then provide copies of the dos and don'ts so you can discuss them and learn together.

- Make a note on your calendar to retake the self-assessments in this chapter a month or two from now. Compare your results to see where you have improved and reflect on what still needs work. Consider sharing your progress on social media or during a staff meeting at the office so your friends and colleagues can celebrate and support you.

"

WISDOM IS YOUR
PERSPECTIVE ON
LIFE, YOUR SENSE
OF BALANCE, YOUR
UNDERSTANDING OF
HOW THE VARIOUS
PARTS AND PRINCIPLES
APPLY AND RELATE TO
EACH OTHER.

"

—Stephen Covey

CHAPTER
5

Strategies for Implementing a Balanced Intervention Visit

So far, you have reflected on EI as a practice, meaning that the work you do requires growth, change, and well, intentional and dedicated practice over time. You have revisited fundamental concepts that, when embedded in the support you provide, result in a balanced approach to supporting both caregiver and child learning. To dive deeper, you explored six adult learning principles and considered what caregivers need to attend, learn, and use intervention strategies with their children. Thinking about how you gather information from families, how you conduct the intake, evaluation and assessment, and how your team writes the IFSP helped connect what you were learning about balanced intervention to the EI process. Now, it's time to sink our teeth into what often feels like the primary activity in EI: the intervention visit.

HOME VISIT VERSUS INTERVENTION VISIT

As I've said before, words matter. They influence how you think, what you say, and the message you convey to others. Since the dawn of time (okay, since the dawn of EI), we have called our activities with families *home visits*. Historically, this made sense, especially when our field switched from primarily center-based service delivery to working with families in natural environments. We moved from playrooms in our office spaces to living rooms in family home spaces. Now, many years later, we still use *home visit* to describe what we do and where it happens. This phrase is ingrained in our thinking, but I think it is time to change what we call our primary activity. If we accept the mission of EI, embracing the idea that our goal is to support caregivers with engaging children in naturally occurring learning opportunities wherever they happen to enhance development, then limiting our vernacular to a *home* visit might not be accurate anymore. With our mission, we support caregivers wherever they are—at the child care center, at grandma's house, on family errands, at the soccer field, in the backyard, and of course in the home—because learning can happen anywhere. According to Part C, Section 303.26 of IDEA 2004, the concept of *natural environments* suggests that EI should happen in places where the family spends time and places where children without delays or disabilities spend time. Both of these ideas emphasize location. Even though our research indicates that visits primarily occur in family homes (Campbell & Sawyer, 2009; Dunst et al., 2014; McWilliam, 2012), I'd like to suggest to you that what we call our work should not focus on location because the location is not what's most important. Stay with me here as I explain.

Let's think more deeply about natural environments. Since its original inclusion in the federal law, this phrase has come to mean more than a location; we now recognize natural environments as a concept that is central to our view of EI practice. This concept expands the context for intervention from simply a place to a perspective. When we provide EI in natural environments, we not only join families in the places that are important to them, but we also join them while doing the things that matter to their family. We join them to figure out how they can use intervention in those places doing those things. It is the intervention that is important, not the place. The concept of natural environments has expanded our thinking beyond location to include the daily routines and activities of families—the contexts in which intervention matters. Natural environments include the interactions with familiar people and materials wherever the child spends time so that intervention can be designed to support those interactions, whether they occur during or between visits. To call this work *home visiting* limits the scope of what EI that aligns with our mission really looks like. Sure, you might think this is semantic, but let's call it what it is. We provide intervention visits that focus on helping caregivers facilitate their children's learning and development wherever it happens. The location (e.g., home) is less important than the interactions between the caregiver and child (i.e., intervention).

One more thing about the difference between a home visit and an intervention visit: If families learn to think about EI as home visiting, they may not consider that we can join them during activities that happen away from the home. They might not know they can ask us to problem-solve with them during a trip to the grocery store where their toddler frequently tantrums. They might also come to think of EI as the home visit, meaning that the magic that happens to transform their child's development occurs during that visit. If, on the other hand, from the earliest contacts families hear that we provide intervention visits that focus on how we can support family interactions that happen anywhere, they might enter the EI system with a broader concept of how support works. We can set the stage for EI that focuses not on a location but on interactions that can include intervention strategies any place, any time. All of this holds true for us too. If you think about what you do as intervention visiting, rather than going to families' homes, it may just expand your perspective.

We provide intervention visits that focus on helping caregivers facilitate their children's learning and development wherever it happens. The location (e.g., home) is less important than the interactions between the caregiver and child (i.e., intervention).

Pause

and REFLECT   *Instructions:* Imagine that you receive a referral call from a new family. Describe how you would explain what EI visits look like so the family gets an idea of what to expect. Or, if you don't typically take referral calls, think about how you would explain EI visits to someone you just met. Review what you wrote and ask yourself: *Does my explanation focus more on the location or what happens during the visit?*

_____

_____

_____

_____

BALANCED INTERVENTION VISIT STRATEGIES

I often think that conducting intervention visits is the great enigma of our field. We have lots of literature about best practices but fewer illustrations of which strategies to use when visiting with families. Our preservice preparation rarely includes much coursework on specifically how to conduct visits, relying instead on readings, videos, and field experiences where students observe visits rather than implement them across much time. Many other practitioners enter the field without ever having learned about or conducted an intervention visit before. All of this contributes to the research-to-practice gap that persists in our field and has an impact on the quality of services families receive. This chapter will try to address this complexity and the practice gap by providing specific strategies you can use to conduct balanced intervention visits that facilitate learning opportunities for both caregivers and children, regardless of where you meet, which goal you are addressing, or your own professional background. That's a tall order, I know, but balanced practices are universal; they apply anytime you walk in the door to visit with a family.

> Balanced practices are universal; they apply anytime
> you walk in the door to visit with a family.

Pause

and REFLECT   *Instructions:* Before moving forward, take a moment to reflect on what you already do now when conducting intervention visits by completing the self-assessment that follows. You can think about a recent visit or think broadly about your EI practices across visits and families. Be sure to capture any thoughts or feelings about your answers in the Notes column. You may want to make a clean copy of the self-assessment before you complete the one here in the book. That way, you have an extra copy you can complete later if you want to compare your answers and track your progress with adopting these practices.

Here is another idea: If you really want to dig deep, share a clean copy of this self-assessment with your supervisor or a colleague. Ask this person to observe you on at least one visit, then complete the assessment about you. Compare your answers to the observer's answers and note where your strengths overlap and any differences between what you think you do and what was observed. The more honest and open to constructive feedback you are, the more likely you will grow from this process.

Self-Assessment: Balanced Intervention Strategies

Item	Never	Not Very Often	Sometimes	Most of the Time	Always	Notes to Explain My Answers
Preparing for the intervention visit						
I review the previous visit's contact note.						
I review the IFSP outcomes.						
I revisit or develop a flexible plan for what we will do during the visit.						
I pause before bringing materials to the visit to consider if they will benefit the caregiver and child and if I can use something already present in the home instead.						
I check in with the caregiver by phone, text, or e-mail.						
Strategies for conducting balanced intervention visits Step 1: Greeting and checking in						
I take responsibility for the energy I bring to the family by entering the visit ready to focus on the child and family.						
I acknowledge each family member when I arrive.						
I follow the caregiver's lead to go where I am needed and join whatever is happening.						
I check in first about the family's life.						

Item	Never	Not Very Often	Sometimes	Most of the Time	Always	Notes to Explain My Answers
I set the stage for what is to come by revisiting the joint plan and being mindful about where I position myself.						
Step 2: Discussion and observation						
I initiate a discussion about the family's priorities, needs, and plans for the visit.						
I actively listen to the caregiver and practice responsiveness to what is said.						
I have reflective conversations to help the caregivers think through what they know, have already tried, or want to change.						
I observe caregiver–child interactions and family routines and activities whenever I can.						
Step 3: Problem solving						
I begin by specifically defining the problem.						
I collaborate with the caregiver to solve the problem by bouncing ideas back and forth.						
I problem-solve with the caregiver in the moment while observing a routine, activity, or interaction.						
After problem solving, I let the caregiver decide which strategy to try with the child.						
Step 4: Practicing the strategy						
I convey the idea to the caregiver that each intervention visit is a practice session for the caregiver and the child.						
I use modeling as a teaching tool to help the caregiver learn to use a strategy.						

(continued)

Item	Never	Not Very Often	Sometimes	Most of the Time	Always	Notes to Explain My Answers
After modeling, I shift the interaction with the child back to the caregiver so the caregiver can practice using the strategy.						
I help the caregiver practice using intervention strategies in real contexts (routines, activities) and in real time.						
I coach the caregiver from the sidelines and intentionally fade my support over time so that the caregiver engages the child with less and less assistance from me.						
I do my best to be patient and celebrate caregiver practice whenever it happens.						
Step 5: Reflection and feedback						
I ask open-ended questions to help the caregiver reflect on prior knowledge and experience with the child.						
I use phrases like "I wonder . . ." to prompt reflection and feedback.						
I invite the caregiver's feedback and share specific feedback with the caregiver about intervention ideas, practice opportunities, observations, etc.						
I am intentional about lowering my ego so I can embrace the caregiver as an equal partner in the child's intervention.						
Step 6: Planning for between visits						
I balance being present during the visit while also focusing on what happens between visits.						
I invite the caregiver's feedback about how the visit went.						
At the end of the visit, I review what was discussed and practiced during the visit with the caregiver.						

Item	Never	Not Very Often	Sometimes	Most of the Time	Always	Notes to Explain My Answers
I let the caregiver decide which strategy(ies) to include on the joint plan for what the caregiver wants to do with the child between visits.						
I provide a written or text copy of the joint plan for the family.						
Step 7: Wrap-up and scheduling						
I plan with the caregiver for what we will do during the next visit.						
I schedule the next visit to accommodate our plan for the activity, routine, or interaction we will address.						
I plan with the caregiver for between-visit check-ins (if helpful).						
I leave the visit with encouraging words and gratitude for being invited into the family's home/life.						

After completing the self-assessment, review your answers and look for patterns. Anywhere you notice a pattern of answers in the Never, Not Very Often, or Sometimes columns, make a note to focus on those steps and strategies as you read the rest of this chapter. Highlight your top three steps or strategies that you want to explore, think and learn more about, and possibly add to your practice. Or, summarize what you notice in one sentence below:

_____

_____

You will refer back to your self-assessment frequently as you move through this chapter. Consider using the self-assessment again in the future, after some of your visits or at certain points in time (in 2 weeks or a month from now) to track your progress with merging these steps and strategies into your professional practice.

Strategies for Preparing for the Intervention Visit

Before you visit with a family, it can be very helpful to dedicate time for preparation. No, I do not mean time to pack your toy bag. Rather, this step involves preparing yourself and helping the family prepare for the visit. It is so easy to bounce from visit to visit during a busy day, assuming you can remember what needs to be done. Taking even 5 minutes to get your head in the game before the visit will help you make sure you are present with the family during the visit. Similarly, checking in with the family before each visit increases the likelihood that caregivers will be physically and mentally available and ready to assume their active roles.

Review the previous visit's contact note. First, make time to review your contact note from the previous visit. I know from experience how easy it is to go from visit to visit without taking time to check in with yourself about what you are supposed to be addressing with the family. You get to know the family well and you get a sense of what is needed. Reviewing your previous contact note will jog your memory about what has been done, what needs to be addressed, and what was planned for the next visit. Reviewing the previous note reminds you of the joint plan you developed with the caregiver at the last visit—the plan that identified what the caregiver planned to do between visits and what you and the caregiver would address at the next visit. (We will discuss joint planning again later.)

Review the IFSP outcomes. The child's and family's outcomes should be listed on your contact note as reference points for documenting progress. Review them before each visit to get grounded in the long-term goals for intervention. Or, if you have not done it in a while (and we are all guilty of this), review the full IFSP. When you really understand child development, it can also be easy to use what you know and follow your own path for what you think the child needs to learn.

Revisiting the IFSP outcomes ensures that you are using what you know to follow the family's path because the outcomes—and the intervention visit—belong to them.

Revisit or develop a flexible plan for what you will do. If a joint plan was developed with the caregiver at the last visit, then revisit the plan in your notes and in your head. Think about what might happen during the planned activity or routine. Consider what you want to observe. Think ahead about how the IFSP outcomes might be addressed. This mental preparation primes you for supporting the caregiver and child. Keep in mind, however, that any plan can get tossed out the window if needs, priorities, or circumstances change so have your plan ready but go into the visit with an open heart and mind. This kind of flexibility is essential in EI practice.

Pause before bringing materials to the visit. Thinking through your flexible plan can lead you to consider bringing materials to the visit. This is a slippery slope in light of the widely accepted idea in our field that toy bags are a big no-no. However, in reality, many EI practitioners still bring toys to visits. Our favorites are books, bubbles, crayons, and maybe even our favorite whistling shape sorter (I really loved that toy. . .). Here's where I stand on bringing toys or materials to intervention visits: Avoid it in favor of using what's in the home (or other environment) because what is already there will continue to be there when you leave. However, I do understand that there are times when bringing something to loan to the family—that's the key, that the family gets to *keep* what you bring—can be beneficial. For instance, if you are a vision specialist, you might have access to a light box or other toys or materials that are less common but could be educational for the child and caregiver. You might be addressing priorities related to motor development and bring materials to make splints or bring a sample seat to try to improve the child's positioning. Or, perhaps you want to bring books because the caregiver mentioned needing them. Whenever the opportunity (or temptation) arises to bring something with you, pause and ask yourself: Am I bringing this item because it will benefit the caregiver and child *or* am

I bringing it because it makes me feel better? If you answer *yes* to the first question, go ahead and bring it but be ready to lend/leave it after practicing with the caregiver how to use the item to encourage the child's development. Be absolutely sure that the item is something the caregiver wants to use rather than something you think he or she should use. Ideally, discuss the item with the caregiver before you bring it. If you bring an item that the caregiver does not want, don't take it personally. Accept rejection gracefully and look for how the caregiver could accomplish the same goal with items the family already has. Or better yet, start there in the first place. Avoid the temptation to bring what is familiar to you and instead explore what is familiar to the family. This is a great way to reinforce the idea that the family has what they need to facilitate the child's development. It also exercises the caregiver's active participation and decision making during the collaborative problem-solving process to identify the item and explore how to use it, presenting a great learning opportunity for both the caregiver and the child.

> Avoid the temptation to bring what is familiar to you and instead, explore what is familiar to the family. If you do bring something, be ready to leave it and loan it to the family.

Now back to our original question—if you really reflect and find that bringing the bubbles makes you feel better (because you are bored, you feel frustrated that the family has few or no toys, you just don't know what else to do), then really dig in there and ask yourself why. What do you need to feel more effective as a service provider? Are you struggling to know what to do with what is already in the environment? Are you struggling to engage the caregiver and/or the child? Process these feelings with a trusted colleague or supervisor. Bring in a mentor on your next visit to help you brainstorm and perhaps see opportunities in the environment you may have missed. I can't say that you should never bring a toy to a visit; just be sure you are doing it for the right reason.

 Check in with the caregiver. Depending on program policies (or your own preferences), you may want to reach out to the caregiver before your next visit. A quick phone call, text, or e-mail can offer a reminder about the date and time of the visit. You can ask if the plan established at the last visit is still appropriate, which serves to touch base in case priorities have changed. Depending on the plan for the next visit, the caregiver might need to prepare too. For example, if you and the caregiver had planned for you to observe the child's behavior during a mealtime, the caregiver probably needs to make sure the child's schedule for the day accommodates this plan so the child does not eat before you arrive. If plans have changed, that's okay. Knowing ahead of time allows both of you the time and space to switch gears.

 I think the key to preparing for an intervention visit is taking what you know from documentation and discussions and intentionally using it to be as mentally and physically ready as possible to support the family. All of your preparation needs to be balanced with a healthy dose of flexibility and patience, knowing that the best laid plans can be thwarted by the tiniest of humans. When plans change, give the caregivers the benefit of the doubt. They are doing the best they can. When plans fall through, consider your part in the planning first. Rather than blame the caregiver for forgetting the joint plan (again—it happens), consider that the plan may have been flawed. Maybe it was your plan and not the caregiver's. Maybe life happened and distracted the family from the plan. Maybe the plan was confusing. Maybe the caregiver really did just forget. Keep in mind that your visit is a small moment in the family's week. You are one part of their big picture. Patience, flexibility, and a balanced approach will help you be an important part of that picture.

All of your preparation needs to be balanced with a healthy dose of flexibility and patience, knowing that the best laid plans can be thwarted by the tiniest of humans.

Throughout this chapter, you will have opportunities to pause and reflect about your practices related to conducting balanced intervention visits. You will think about your EI visits with families and use these reflection points to identify which strategies you already use and which you want to add to your practices. Your self-assessment will come in handy as you drill down into your practices to examine them through the lens of balanced intervention. After you identify any new strategies you want to embrace, you will create an action plan that specifically describes how you plan to integrate the strategy into your work. I encourage you to come back to this book after using the new strategy to describe your experience using what you learned. This mindful approach to examining your professional development will help you extend your commitment to facilitating balanced intervention beyond the pages of this book.

Pause and REFLECT

Describe how you prepared for your most recent visit:

_____

_____

_____

_____

When preparing for this visit, I:

❏ Reviewed the previous visit's contact note

❏ Reviewed the IFSP outcomes

❏ Revisited or developed a flexible plan for what I hoped to do during the visit

❏ Paused before bringing materials to the visit

❏ Checked in with the caregiver

If you identified a strategy you want to add to your practice, describe your action plan for how you will use it. Be specific, then come back later to note your experience.

Action plan: _____

Experience using the strategy while facilitating balanced intervention:

_____

_____

SEVEN STEPS AND TONS OF STRATEGIES FOR CONDUCTING BALANCED INTERVENTION VISITS

Visiting families is what we do. It is how, when, and where we provide our support. The span of time between the initial IFSP meeting and the child's eventual transition out of the EI system (what I call IFSP implementation) is where we spend the majority of our energy with families, so it is important to be mindful of what we do. We get to choose how we spend that energy—whether we plop on the living room floor and play with the child for 45 minutes or we function as a member of a triad and balance our intention and attention on learning experiences for both the child and the caregiver. The strategies in this section will give you some ideas about how to conduct balanced intervention visits using what you have learned in the previous chapters. I have organized the strategies within a seven-step framework for conducting EI visits that I introduced in *Family-Centered Early Intervention* (Childress, 2015). Even if you are an experienced service provider, it can be helpful to have a framework to organize the flow of your visits. I use the word *flow* because any framework for EI practice cannot be strict; it has to flow to adjust and accommodate the circumstances of each family and each visit. Although I would recommend you use all seven of the steps, you may find that you don't need to use all of the strategies in this section on each visit, and that's okay. Just set your intention to use as many as possible and tweak them to fit your style.

Step 1: Greeting and Checking In

First things first—before you greet the family, take a moment to set your intention. Enter the visit mindfully, with the goal and the mission of EI in mind. Quickly do a mental scan to review what you did to prepare for this specific visit. Make sure your mobile device is set for vibrate or mute so that you will be fully present with the family. Now, you are ready to knock on the door.

Strategies for Greeting and Checking In

Take responsibility for the energy you bring to the family. While setting your intention for the visit, start by taking a deep, cleansing breath to prepare you to leave behind whatever stresses or frustrations you had before the visit. Enter the environment in a frame of mind that will allow you to focus on what the child and family need. This can be easier said than done on hectic days with cancellations or personal distractions, but remember that you would want a service provider for yourself or your child who is present and focused, not hurried or distracted. Be that person for each family. I think Dr. Jill Bolte Taylor summed it up perfectly when she said, "Please take responsibility for the energy you bring to me" (Oprah.com, 2011).

Acknowledge each member of the family. As you enter the environment, greet whomever you see. Say "hi" to the caregiver, acknowledge all of the children, and introduce yourself to any new family members or friends. You can just shake hands and say your name if you are worried about confidentiality. Create an atmosphere of genuine friendliness and respect and you will be more likely to receive that in return.

Follow the caregiver's lead. Remember, if you are visiting the family's home, you are a guest. Scan the environment and follow the caregiver's lead. For instance, you may notice that there are shoes piled by the front door and the family members are in bare feet. Ask if you should remove your shoes. If you notice that the caregiver always takes you to a certain room, let him or her know that you can join them wherever they are most comfortable, wherever they were before you arrived. Following the caregiver's lead means keeping an open mind and a flexible presence to go where you are needed and join whatever is happening.

Check in first about the family's life. Take a few moments to ask about how the caregiver and family are. You may be tempted to jump straight to reviewing the previous joint plan, but acknowledging the caregiver as a fellow human first can break down walls and build rapport, especially with a new family or a caregiver who is reluctant to engage. If the caregiver previously shared a personal challenge, check in about that but be careful to maintain professional boundaries. This is another thing that requires a careful balance, being friendly without being friends. We do not want to become friends with a family because that could compromise our objectivity and make it harder for the family to address concerns with us or about us to the service coordinator. Check in, show you remember what's important to the caregiver, and show you care, but be mindful of boundaries as you do.

> Acknowledging the caregiver as a fellow human first can break down walls and build rapport, especially with a new family or a caregiver who is reluctant to engage.

Set the stage for what's to come. As you transition from greeting to intervention, use the joint plan to ground you. Revisit the previous visit's joint plan with a specific question that highlights the strategy the caregiver was planning to implement, such as "How did it go with using music to help Amber settle down at naptime?" Be sure your question is open-ended; avoid asking if the caregiver implemented the joint plan (yes/no question + jargon of "joint plan" = shoulder shrug or a caregiver who is put on the spot). Use your body to set the stage too. Pay attention to where you sit or stand so that you position yourself to support the caregiver's learning as well. For example, rather than plopping down in front of the toddler and reaching for a toy, try sitting beside the caregiver and asking what she and the child have been up to that day. Or, sit so that you are one point in the intervention triangle, establishing the triad that includes you, the caregiver, and the child, from the beginning. Another option is to start by sitting next to the caregiver and letting her guide where you go next. If the caregiver is on the couch, start there. If the caregiver is at the kitchen table, check in there and then transition to a discussion about what she wants to do during today's visit. This helps the caregiver understand that you are not just there for the child; you are there as a support and partner to her too.

Pause
and REFLECT *Instructions:* Describe the first 10 minutes of your most recent visit. Consider what strategies you used to greet the family and check in before jumping into intervention.

How did I begin the visit?

_____

_____

_____

During this time, I:

☐ Took responsibility for the energy I brought to the family by making sure I was ready to focus on the child and family from the beginning

☐ Acknowledged each family member

☐ Followed the caregiver's lead

☐ Checked in with the caregiver about how the family was doing

☐ Set the stage for what was to come by:

  ● Revisiting the previous session's joint plan

  ● Being mindful about where I positioned myself

Action plan for using a new strategy:

Experience using the strategy while facilitating balanced intervention:

Step 2: Discussion and Observation

After checking in, you or the caregiver will probably move the conversation in the direction of intervention. This discussion sometimes develops out of the joint plan discussion or from the mention of a new skill or challenge. Use the strategies you learned in Chapter 4 to nurture your relationship with the caregiver, facilitate information sharing, and have a reflective conversation. Based on what you learn from the discussion, seize opportunities to observe caregiver–child interactions to see what they like, what they don't like, what goes well, and what is a struggle. Step 2 is an important one that can be unintentionally skipped in our eagerness to jump in and "help," so make sure you take time for it.

Discussion and Observation Strategies

Open a discussion about priorities, needs, and plans for the visit. If this does not naturally occur from revisiting the joint plan, you may need to initiate a discussion about what the caregiver wants to do during the visit. You can check in on previous family priorities and needs or simply ask, "What would you like to do today?" or "How can I help you and Amber today?" Listen for information that describes what is most immediately relevant and what would be useful to the caregiver (EI Adult Learning Principle 1). Follow that lead and ask the caregiver, "Would you like some help with that?" Even better, ask if you can see the activity that goes well or challenges the family. This kind of discussion can naturally shift into a rich observation and an opportunity to problem-solve together.

Listen for information that describes what is most immediately relevant and
what would be useful to the caregiver, and then follow that lead.

Actively listen and practice responsiveness. This might go without saying but let's
say it anyway. Show the caregiver you are invested in the discussion by leaning in and
making eye contact. Be responsive by using affirmative feedback ("I hear you," "That
sounds really hard," "I'm glad you shared that," "Okay, so it sounds like Amber is. . .") to
let the caregiver know you are with him or her. Communicate your thoughtful attention and you will find caregivers more willing to share. Think about when you were at
a doctor's appointment or some other meeting with a professional where that person
seemed distracted, hurried, or like he or she was barely paying attention. Remember
how you felt—devalued, frustrated, dismissed. There really is no excuse for that kind
of behavior.

Being present, invested, attentive, and responsive are all
part of a mindful approach to family support.

Have a reflective conversation. A reflective conversation helps the caregiver think
through what she knows, has already tried, needs to know, or wants to change (EI Adult
Learning Principle 2). It allows you to gather information and helps the caregiver think
about the issue at hand. It is also a great lead-in to observation and problem solving.
Remember to take that perspective of discovery that I talked about in Chapter 4. If you
find yourself suggesting strategies or jumping in to engage the child right away, you are
not having a reflective conversation. If, instead, you ask those open-ended questions
without assuming you know the answers, you will be facilitating a thinking process that
respects the expertise the caregiver brings to intervention rather than barreling over it
in favor of your own opinions. Pause and make space to learn about what the caregiver
thinks, understands, and has experienced. Avoid judgment and maintain an attitude of
respect, believing that your role is to build on what the caregiver knows and does. This
can be a huge shift for you if you are used to diving right in with the child, doing lots of
modeling, or instantly accessing that huge resource file in your head. Taking the time to
listen rather than spew suggestions to a problem you can't possibly fully understand yet
will make a world of difference.

    Observe whenever you can. Observation is another skill that takes time to prac-
tice and even remember to use. During the discussion, you might hear about a successful or problematic routine. Seize the moment and use the "show me" prompt to ask for
permission to observe the routine. Ask the caregiver, "How do you feel about showing
me how you use that strategy?" or "I would love to see that. Could you show me?" Or,
your observation might be more subtle. You might end up observing a caregiver–child
interaction or a child behavior during the discussion that provides you with information you need or offers an opportunity to use an intervention strategy. If it won't hurt
rapport, sometimes it can be okay to interrupt the discussion to point out the opportunity for observation and practice. Imagine that you see Amber opening a cabinet in the
kitchen. You might ask her mother about what Amber is doing and seize the opportunity to practice prompting her to make choices from snacks when it is most relevant to

Amber. You could start by asking if you could watch what the mother would typically do in this situation. This is so important because you need to see the norm before you can build on it. Then, perhaps you could support the mother in implementing strategies that were previously discussed, such as holding a snack up by her face to model the item's name for Amber, using wait time for Amber to imitate the word, or offering a choice of two snacks and then labeling the snack Amber picks. Be on the lookout for natural learning opportunities like this because they take advantage of several of our EI adult learning principles and make learning motivating for the child (and often the caregiver too).

Seize the moment and use the "show me" prompt to
ask for permission to observe the routine.

Observation can also be helpful when introducing a new intervention strategy. You might describe it to the caregiver then encourage her to try it with her child. For some families, trying out a new strategy while you observe can be a great way to receive support. Other caregivers might want you to try the strategy first (i.e., model it for them). We'll talk more about modeling in a moment. Just keep in mind that early in the process, observing the caregiver and child should be your goal rather than starting by having the caregiver observe you. When in doubt, however, ask. Ask if the caregiver is comfortable trying a strategy while you watch. Provide the choice to watch you first like this: "Would you like to try that strategy with Amber or would you rather watch me use it first?" If you have created a safe space for the caregiver, then it will be more likely that he or she will be comfortable being observed.

Pause

and REFLECT   *Instructions:* Use the space below to think critically about your use of discussion and observation during visits. Think about two visits: one where the discussion stays on topic and observation is easy, and another where you experience the opposite. Note any differences in which strategies you used during these visits and any you want to add to your practice.

Visit 1: Discussion stayed on topic and observation was easy

Visit 2: Challenging discussion and observation, what observation?

During Visit 1, I:

❑ Initiated a discussion about family priorities, needs, and plans for the visit

❑ Actively listened to the caregiver and practiced responsiveness

❑ Had a reflective conversation to help the caregiver access prior knowledge and experience

❑ Observed caregiver–child interactions, routines, or activities

Which of these four strategies did you use or not use during Visit 2? Why or why not?

_____

_____

_____

Action plan for using a new strategy:

_____

Experience using the strategy while facilitating balanced intervention:

_____

_____

Step 3: Problem Solving

Collaborative problem solving can occur before, during, or after a discussion or observation. It can happen during a discussion when the need arises to define a problem and identify possible strategies. Or, it can occur during or after an observation when the use of a strategy is unsuccessful or does not result in the desired outcome. Problem solving can be helpful when you need to tweak a strategy, identify an alternative strategy, or think through how to use a strategy in a different way or during a different routine.

The key to problem solving is that it is a collaborative, reciprocal process.

Problem-Solving Strategies

Define the problem. Begin by making sure you really understand the problem. If a grandmother tells you that her grandson will not eat, you might think you know the problem, but without actually defining it, you could be way off. Ask the caregiver to describe what the child does, what the caregiver does, and what any other family members do during the routine or activity. Get specific. Observe the problem, if possible, in person or on video. Once you have a clear picture, ask the caregiver what he or she envisions the routine looking like if it went perfectly well. That will give you direction for the intervention.

Bounce ideas back and forth. Once you understand the problem, it's time for some collaborative problem solving. This involves a reciprocal sharing of ideas about strategies the caregiver can use to address the problem or build the child's skills. It is not a one-way spouting of ideas where you tell the caregiver what to do—so resist the urge to take control here to shift the balance in your direction. Instead, listen for what is most relevant and important to the caregiver (EI Adult Learning Principle 1) even if it is not on the IFSP. Reflect and think together about what the caregiver has already tried (EI Adult Learning Principle 2) to solve the problem so you don't waste time with suggestions that the caregiver already knows will not work.

Problem-solve in the moment. Whenever possible, problem-solve with the caregiver in context and in real time (EI Adult Learning Principle 5). While observing the routine or activity, share what you notice, listen to the caregiver's intuition, and work together to brainstorm strategies to try. Problem solving in the moment gets entangled with practicing intervention strategies, but that is a good thing. When you can problem-solve together, coach the caregiver through practicing a strategy, then wrap back to reflection, do more problem solving if needed, and share feedback, you will have a balanced system in place that truly promotes collaboration and learning for all.

> Problem solving in the moment gets entangled with practicing intervention strategies, but that is a good thing.

Let the caregiver decide which strategy to try. Observation and problem solving get you closer to the active participation and practice that is so integral to caregiver learning (EI Adult Learning Principle 4). After you and the caregiver have tossed around ideas, shared feedback about observations, and discussed options, encourage the caregiver to decide which strategy fits best to address the original need. Rather than your choosing, give the caregiver the opportunity to make an informed decision about the strategy and how to use it. After all, he or she will make these decisions without you most of the time so why not facilitate this thinking process during the visit?

Pause
and REFLECT   *Instructions:* Think about a recent visit during which you helped the caregiver think through a problem. Consider how you used or could have used the strategies you just learned.

During my visit, problem solving looked/sounded like this:

_____

_____

_____

When we problem solved, I:

- ❑ Began by specifically defining the problem
- ❑ Collaborated with the caregiver by bouncing ideas back and forth
- ❑ Problem-solved in the moment while observing
- ❑ Let the caregiver decide which strategy to try with the child

Action plan for using a new strategy:

_____

Experience using the strategy while facilitating balanced intervention:

_____

_____

Step 4: Practicing the Strategy

This step is such an important part of the process. Facilitating the caregiver's active participation and practice (EI Adult Learning Principle 4) is essential to spreading the learning beyond the EI visit. To do this, you will be looking for and seizing opportunities to implement the four interventions you learned about in Chapter 2. You will be looking for and helping the caregiver identify the naturally occurring learning opportunities that already exist or could exist in the child's and family's daily interactions and environment that could be used to enhance the child's development (Intervention 1). You will use those opportunities to strengthen caregiver–child relationships and the caregiver's responsiveness to the child through the support you provide within the context of the intervention triad (Intervention 2). When you use each visit as a practice opportunity for the caregiver to try out intervention strategies with the child, you will be building the caregiver's awareness of the power of his or her interactions with the child (Intervention 3). Through reflection and feedback, you will also help the caregiver interpret his or her own actions so that the caregiver can make adjustments to help the child achieve the outcomes that are important to the family (Intervention 3 again). Finally, if you are embracing what you have been learning in this book, you will understand that your goal with any intervention visit is to facilitate active caregiver participation, reflection, and decision making while the caregiver engages the child, adapts intervention strategies, and plans for what to do between visits (Intervention 4). That may sound like a lot to accomplish in any one visit, but facilitating practice with these ideas in mind is so important to adult learning. You already know it is essential for child learning. Let's combine the two so that both learners get what they need during your visits.

With all of that said, I think it is important to acknowledge that facilitating caregiver practice can also be one of the hardest things to do during a visit. Some caregivers are ready to dive right in and able to receive your support from some of the earliest visits. Other caregivers struggle to "let you in" to their daily life and see you as a partner rather than an expert for whom they must clear a path and get out of the way. Whether caregivers feel comfortable with practicing a strategy in front of you depends on many variables, such as the relationship you have built and how new or well-developed it is; the caregiver's personality, cultural values, and personal preferences; the family's stress level; the caregiver's understanding of his or her active role in the child's intervention; the sense of vulnerability and safety the caregiver feels; and your own skills with providing family support. You do not have control over all of these variables, but you can stack the deck in your favor by focusing on what you can do to make practicing a safe and beneficial experience for all.

Strategies for Facilitating Caregiver Practice

Convey the idea that each intervention visit is a practice session for the caregiver and child. Absorb this idea and use it when you are setting your intention before you knock on the door. Examine your own beliefs to see how this idea matches or does not match with what you were taught in school. If it matches, great! If it does not match, sit with the idea for a while. Compare it to what you learned or what you have previously believed. Ask yourself what it would take to evolve your beliefs to match with this idea that you are an EI service provider who provides balanced intervention that focuses on learning for caregivers and children. Beliefs are hard to change, but with purposeful effort (like your work here in this book), you can do it.

At your first visit, explain how EI visits work with this idea in mind. Reiterate this idea frequently because, remember, it takes time for caregivers to establish their understanding of how EI works. Use the word *practice* often, as in "What would you like to practice today?" or "How do you feel about practicing that strategy with Amber while I'm here?" Coach the caregiver through the practice and ask how practicing felt. When the visit veers away from practice, such as when the child engages you more than the caregiver, the caregiver's attention is diverted, or your modeling has moved into child-focused intervention, notice this and gently steer yourself and the interactions back toward caregiver–child practice.

> Use the word *practice* often, as in "What would you like to practice today?" or "How do you feel about practicing that strategy with Amber while I'm here?"

Use modeling as a teaching tool. Check in with yourself about what you call "modeling" and how often you model. I have noticed that many of us use *modeling* to describe (or maybe excuse) the amount of time we actually spend engaging the child. If you tend to spend most of your visit modeling with the child, then consider whom are you modeling for. If you are truly modeling to support the caregiver's learning, then modeling will be brief and purposeful. It will also almost always be followed by caregiver practice. If what you call modeling means you are playing with, stretching, or prompting the child for most of the visit, then an honest reevaluation of how your support aligns with the goal and mission of EI is probably needed. Let's look at some strategies for modeling to help you identify the difference.

- *Ask for permission to model first.* When it is appropriate, ask if you can try something with the child first to see if it will work. It is perfectly acceptable to try a strategy using your expertise. Just remember that when you use the strategy successfully first, and the caregiver struggles to replicate it, you might do damage to the caregiver's confidence. Sometimes, this can be avoided by asking if the caregiver wants to try first and offering your support through coaching rather than feeling the need to be the one to lead the attempt.

- *Describe what you will model and what to watch for.* Describe the strategy you plan to model, why it might be beneficial to the child's development, and how you plan to use it (EI Adult Learning Principle 3). This will orient the caregiver as a learner, priming him or her for an active learning experience (EI Adult Learning Principle 4). The alternative is a caregiver who passively watches you engage the child while you model.

> Passive observation does not lend itself to active learning, so whenever you can, give the caregiver an active role during your modeling.

- *Describe what you are doing while modeling.* Be specific and narrate what you do with the child while you do it. Call attention to what you say and do, how you use your hands, or how you position the child. Use common language, avoiding jargon and technical terminology.

- *After modeling, ask the caregiver for feedback.* Talk about what the caregiver saw you do and what he or she saw the child do. Connect the dots with the caregiver between what you did and the outcome. Ask the caregiver how this compares to what the caregiver usually does, but do this gently because you do not want to offend.

- *Shift from modeling to caregiver practice.* Always shift the interaction with the child back to the caregiver after a modeling episode. Ask, "Would you like to try it now?" and be accepting of the answer. If the answer is frequently "no," then consider a different way to offer the practice opportunity. For example, a better way to make this shift is to use an open-ended question such as, "What do you think about trying that strategy with Amber?" Or, you can use a statement that assumes caregiver participation, such as, "Mommy's turn!" while you pass the spoon to the mother after modeling a feeding strategy. Establish this as a balanced caregiver support routine so that whenever you use modeling, you always intentionally facilitate active caregiver learning before, during, and afterward.

> Establish this as a balanced caregiver support routine so that whenever you use modeling, you always intentionally facilitate active caregiver learning before, during, and afterward.

Pause
to Practice   *Instructions:* Read the two scenarios and consider how the different interpretations of modeling connect to the mission of EI, represent the intervention triad, and illustrate balanced intervention. As you read, be mindful of your reactions and ask yourself: *Which scenario more closely represents my style of modeling?*

Scenario 1: Ebony has been working with Casey and her son Kyle for several weeks now. On their most recent visit, Ebony modeled strategies to encourage Kyle's motor development because learning to walk was Casey's main goal for her son. Ebony moved toys up to the couch, along the edge, and down to the floor to encourage Kyle to pull himself to stand, cruise along the couch, and lower himself back to the floor. She described what she was doing as she helped Kyle use a half kneel to pull to stand and then held Kyle at the hips to guide him as he lowered back to the floor. Ebony explained that this game would help Kyle build strength in his legs and trunk and help with coordination. Casey cheered for Kyle as he moved, and she called his name when it looked like Kyle was going to let go of the couch to take a step in Casey's direction. Ebony asked Casey if she thought she could play this game during the week, and Casey said she thought so. They wrote it on the joint plan as they wrapped up the visit. During the week, however, Kyle was not interested in cruising along the couch and would pull to stand and then quickly plop back down to the floor. Casey felt frustrated because she had seen Kyle do this so easily with Ebony. She wondered, "What am I doing wrong?"

Which modeling strategies did Ebony use?

❏   Asked Casey for permission to model first

❏   Described what she was going to model and what Casey should watch for

❏   Described what she was doing while modeling the strategy with Kyle

❏   After modeling, she asked Casey for feedback

❏   Shifted from modeling to offer Casey the opportunity to practice using the strategy with Kyle

Which modeling strategies were missing? If Ebony had used these strategies, how might they have helped prepare Casey for how to support Kyle during this activity between visits?

_____

_____

Scenario 2: At her next visit, Ebony asks Casey, "How did Kyle do with moving along the couch?" Casey says that Kyle was stubborn and kept plopping back down when he pulled himself up so he didn't really cruise. Ebony thinks back to last week's visit and realizes that she did not give Casey the opportunity to practice with Kyle. She asks Casey to show her what she tried so she could see what Kyle does. Casey put Kyle by the couch and put Kyle's hands on the cushion. Kyle pulled to stand by rolling over his toes, saw that there was no toy on the cushion, and then sat back down on the carpet. Ebony revisited what worked last week and wondered with Casey about what might motivate Kyle to stay standing. Casey says that Kyle loves his new musical toy and has started swaying to the music. Ebony encourages Casey to put the toy up on the couch and then start the music. Kyle immediately looks up and starts to pull himself to stand. Ebony asks if she can show Casey how to help Kyle stand using a half kneel instead of rolling over his toes and Casey says yes. Ebony asks Casey to watch where she puts her hands on Kyle's lower trunk and hips. She shifts Kyle's weight to the left and helps him bend his right leg so his foot is flat on the floor. Ebony then puts both hands back on Kyle's hips to guide him as he stands up. After modeling, she asks Casey what she noticed. Casey says she liked how Ebony helped Kyle get his foot in the right spot so he could stand up. Ebony asks Casey if she would like to try and Casey says, "Sure!" Casey sits Kyle back down, restarts the music, and then guides Kyle onto his knees. When Kyle tries to stand by only using his arms to pull himself up, Ebony coaches Casey through how to shift Kyle's weight and then get his leg bent with his foot on the floor. Casey successfully moves Kyle through the position and cheers when Kyle stands up and pats his toy. Ebony and Casey talk through how it felt to move Kyle from sitting to standing. Casey practices two more times, and then they let Kyle play with his toy while they talk about how to help Kyle learn to lower himself back down to the floor. They practice strategies to help Kyle lower himself slowly to the floor instead of plopping back down. When they write the joint plan, Casey decides to practice helping Kyle use a half kneel to pull up and lower himself from the couch each morning when they play after breakfast. She plans to show her partner how to do this, too, so she can work with Kyle in the evenings.

Which modeling strategies did Ebony use this time?

❏   Asked Casey for permission to model first

❏   Described what she was going to model and what Casey should watch for

❏   Described what she was doing while modeling the strategy with Kyle

❏   After modeling, she asked Casey for feedback

❏   Shifted from modeling to offer Casey the opportunity to practice using the strategy with Kyle

Which strategies were missing? _____

Which scenario was more likely to build Casey's confidence with knowing how to help her son? Why?

_____

_____

Which scenario more closely matches your intervention style? _____

If Scenario 1 felt more familiar to you, revisit a recent opportunity when you modeled a strategy for a family. Use the space that follows to rewrite the opportunity by imagining how it might have worked if you had used all of the modeling strategies. Keep this in mind on your next visit and set a goal to model with intention.

_____

_____

_____

_____

Practice in real contexts and in real time. Whenever the opportunity arises for you to join a typical family activity or routine during the visit, take it. Practicing the use of an intervention strategy in context and in real time (EI Adult Learning Principle 5) may be the most important thing you can do to prepare the caregiver to use intervention strategies between visits. Your presence always changes a routine or activity so do your best to help the family replicate what would happen naturally. That way, you get to see the interactions that provide the natural learning opportunities for the child's development and build on them rather than try to create new ones that may or may not fit within the family's life. You also get to support the caregiver in using an intervention strategy in the context in which he or she will use it beyond the visit. As you know by now, this is essential for caregiver learners to generalize what they learn beyond the visit and maintain that learning across time. Think about it this way: Learning the names of animals in a book is okay if a family has books and enjoys looking at them, but learning the names of animals on a family's farm is much more meaningful to a child who tags along with her grandfather in the mornings to feed the goats, pigs, and chickens.

Opportunities to support the caregiver's practice during a real routine (i.e., context) may arise spontaneously during the visit or they may need to be planned. Which contexts you can join and which activities and routines are available in real time will vary, but your focus on supporting balanced practice for both the caregiver and the child should remain consistent. Here are a few specific strategies to help you keep your focus.

- *Seize a spontaneous opportunity for practice.* To seize on a spontaneous activity or routine during your visit, you first have to notice it. This requires attention to what is happening around you and the ability to be an observer while you are working with the family. When you notice a golden opportunity, describe what you see and ask the caregiver about it. Ask if the three of you can try out the intervention strategy in this spontaneous activity or routine. If the caregiver agrees, then provide verbal guidance about how to try the strategy during the activity if the caregiver seems unsure about what to do. Do your very best to avoid stepping into the routine first unless the caregiver asks to watch you use the strategy. If you need to model, do so once and then step out of the routine and let the caregiver take over. Sometimes, you might need to simply observe the caregiver's first attempt without providing guidance, just to let the caregiver try the strategy. Other times, you might need to provide guidance during the practice. This often depends on the relationship you have built with the caregiver and on the caregiver's preferences. If you are not sure whether to provide guidance during the activity or wait until after, just ask.

> To seize on a spontaneous activity or routine during your visit, you first have to notice it. This requires attention to what is happening around you, the ability to be an observer while you are working with the family.

- *Plan for practicing in context and in real time.* Sometimes, the context in which practice makes the most sense requires some planning, such as when you join the family during a trip to the community pool to help the caregiver practice range of motion exercises with the child in the warm water. Planning gives the caregiver time to prepare for you to join the activity, which may make the practice opportunity more comfortable for the family. The trick with joining a planned activity is to treat it like a spontaneous opportunity as much as possible. Let the caregiver know that you want to observe first to see what he or she would normally do if you were not present. Then, you can discuss what you observed, brainstorm and problem-solve together about how to use intervention strategies, and then support the caregiver and child as they practice together. You can maintain the intervention triad in any situation to provide support, and then ease yourself out of the routine so the caregiver practices with the child more naturally, with less and less support. This is the same whether the practice opportunity was spontaneous or planned.

- *Notice micro-routines.* Sometimes, what I call *micro-routines* can pop up that offer fantastic opportunities for the caregiver to use an intervention strategy and the child to practice a skill. These routines are *micro* because they are pieces of larger routines that can easily be missed. For instance, we often talk about common routines like mealtimes, playtime, dressing, or bath time. Each of these routines has micro-routines within them that are often unique to the family. For instance, how a caregiver and child get ready for bath time is probably unique to them. You would need to find out how bath time is announced to the child. Ask what each person does before, during, and after the bath. How does the child get into the tub? What does the child do while being bathed? Does the child play with any toys in the water? How does the micro-routine of ending the bath and getting dry happen? Observing, or at least talking about, these micro-routines can provide a great way to help the caregiver think about these important and subtle interactions that influence child development. When you break down a routine into its micro components (think about task analysis), you can help the caregiver learn to analyze and identify the key components that either make a routine problematic or full of opportunities.

> When you break down a routine into its micro components (think about task analysis), you can help the caregiver learn to analyze and identify the key components that either make a routine problematic or full of opportunities.

Tweaking a micro-routine can make all the difference. Let me tell you a true bath time story. William's grandmother told me that bath time was the absolute worst time of day. William would cry from the moment the water was turned on until he was dressed after the bath. I was not able to observe bath time (because it was typically around 8 p.m.), so we talked through the routine in detail. After discussing what happened before, during, and after bath time and what each person did, we discovered that the most difficult part was getting William out of the tub. He would cry before his bath, then settle down in the water, and then scream when it was time to get out. This routine had been going on for months, but initially, William only became upset at the end. When I asked the grandmother to tell me specifically how she transitioned William out of the tub (micro-routine), we discovered that the turning point came when she picked William up out of the warm water. She would tell him bath time was over and scoop him up. He would scream and thrash, which was dangerous for them both because he was slippery. We came up with the simple idea of giving William time to ease out of the tub by letting him pull the plug. He could continue to play while the water drained, and then he was likely to feel cold and be more motivated to get out of the tub. We also discussed letting him climb out of the tub himself to stand on the rug rather than being picked up. His grandmother liked these ideas, so they became part of her joint plan. At the next week's visit, she met me at the door celebrating her success. Draining the water and letting William climb out of the tub completely changed the dynamic. He had some control, she was no longer frustrated, and bath time became a scream-free zone. What a success, and it all came down to a micro-routine.

Pause

and REFLECT and PLAN   *Instructions:* Think of a routine or activity you recently observed or joined. Or, think about one a caregiver recently mentioned. Dissect what you know about the routine and identify each micro-routine in the following chart. Add ideas for intervention strategies that could be used during the micro-routine(s) to address the child's development and work toward IFSP outcomes. Note which micro-routine you want to discuss or observe on your next visit.

Child/family routine:			
Micro-routine:	Micro-routine	Micro-routine	Micro-routine
Intervention strategy:	Intervention strategy:	Intervention strategy:	Intervention strategy:
❑ Observe or discuss at the next visit	❑ Observe or discuss at the next visit	❑ Observe or discuss at the next visit	❑ Observe or discuss at the next visit

Tip: Use this chart (or create your own) to help you and the caregiver break down a challenging routine into its micro-routines. Together, look for opportunities when the caregiver could use an intervention strategy to improve the routine or help the child learn or practice a new skill. You can also use this chart to examine an enjoyable routine to identify what works well and where intervention strategies might fit.

Coach from the sidelines and fade your support over time. Again, whenever you can coach from the sidelines without injecting yourself in or directly interfering with a routine or caregiver–child interaction, you are more likely to facilitate authentic practice that the caregiver can replicate between visits without you. This might involve providing verbal guidance, gestures, and/or even modeling using a prop (such as a doll). When you use verbal cues, be specific but gentle in your execution. You never want to "boss" the caregiver around or be too directive, so be mindful of your tone of voice and pacing. When you do need to jump into a routine, perhaps to use hand-over-hand guidance or provide support to the child, ease yourself back out when you can so the natural routine can reestablish itself. Or, if you need to provide a great deal of support during the first practice, fade your support over subsequent practices to get closer to how the caregiver will use the strategy between visits.

When coaching, try to let the routine or interaction happen. Be there for support and don't be afraid to provide guidance, but remember to be mindful about the effect your presence can have. I remember a visit during which I was trying to coach a mother to encourage her son's communication and feeding during breakfast. I struggled to figure out how to coach her because the child was so distracted by trying to engage me. I tried sitting behind the child, but he spun around. I tried ignoring him but I'm sure you can imagine how unsuccessful that was. We all ended up laughing, which was great for our rapport but not so great for the practice session. I ended up backing into the living room and peeking around the corner to watch the routine after the child was engaged with his mother.

After she tried the strategy, we chatted a bit and then I backed out of the room so she could try again. It felt a bit clunky to me at first, but with a sense of humor and some flexibility, we found a way to make the practice work.

Be patient and celebrate practice whenever it happens. We know that practice is essential, and when we set the stage for intervention, we do our best to emphasize this to families so they understand the importance of their participation. Hopefully, this will be enough, along with the caregiver's motivation to help the child, to ensure that practice happens during visits. You and I both know that for many families, that is enough to hit the ground running, but for other families, it takes time to achieve. We must be patient with how practice happens for a family and give them time, when they need it, to become more comfortable. How often practice happens and what it looks like will vary across families and visits. Practice might happen across multiple episodes on each visit or we might celebrate a single 10-minute episode of caregiver practice with the child. Celebrate practice whenever it happens and help caregivers see the results of their efforts. Next time, try to extend the practice a few more minutes, a few more turns, or even one more try. When practice is unsuccessful, talk about it. Explore it with the caregiver to find out if there is something you can change to make it work better in the future. If practice opportunities are few and far between, reflect on why that might be. It can be so easy to "blame" the caregiver for not wanting to practice, not paying attention, or not talking to her child but, truly, blame never gets you anywhere. Instead of blaming, keep your mind on seizing caregiver practice opportunities but be kind to yourself when circumstances are challenging. Avoid blaming the family for struggles you feel; instead, acknowledge the struggle, reflect a bit, and then plan for next time.

Sometimes, when I feel deflated after a visit because the practice opportunities were few and far between, I have found that writing my contact note right away helps me see what went well during the visit and how rich the interaction actually was. I have also found that caregivers who struggle with practice often find what they did practice is the one thing they want to list on their joint plan. Practice has value, even when it is hard, so keep your chin up and know that every moment of practice for the caregiver and child is a moment to celebrate.

Pause
and REFLECT   *Instructions:* Practice—what does that mean to you? What does it look like on your visits? Reflect on another recent visit and think about a specific caregiver practice episode. Consider what you did, what the caregiver did, and what the child did. Think about what you did before, during, and after the practice episode too.

Before—How we prepared for and entered into caregiver practice:

_____

_____

During—What I did to support the caregiver during practice:

_____

_____

After—How the caregiver practice episode ended:

_____

_____

When I facilitated caregiver practice during this visit, I:

❑ Conveyed the idea that each visit is a practice session for the caregiver and child (or had previously shared this with the caregiver)

❑ Used modeling as a teaching tool to help the caregiver learn to use the new strategy

❑ Shifted the interaction with the child back to the caregiver so he or she could practice using the strategy I modeled

❑ Helped the caregiver practice using the strategy in real contexts and in real time

❑ Coached from the sidelines and faded my support over time

❑ Did my best to be patient and celebrate caregiver practice whenever it happened

Action plan for using a new strategy:

_____

Experience using the strategy while facilitating balanced intervention:

_____

_____

Step 5: Reflection and Feedback

Reflection and feedback often occur during and/or after a practice episode. When we reflect with caregivers, we help them consider the connection between their interactions, actions, and words and their child's behavior and learning. Recognizing this link is essential to successful intervention. Feedback also plays a part here because it is your opportunity to share your observations about that connection. Feedback can be a teaching tool for the caregiver when you raise awareness and a tool for you when the caregiver gives you feedback. I believe that reflection and feedback are both reciprocal processes. If either only works one way, such as if you only asked open-ended questions or you only provided feedback, then the shared exchange of ideas that is so important to EI will not happen. Be ready to reflect and share feedback *with* the caregiver and receive feedback from the caregiver to enhance your intervention support (EI Adult Learning Principle 6).

Feedback can be a teaching tool for the caregiver when you raise awareness and a tool for you when the caregiver gives you feedback.

Reflection and Feedback Strategies

Ask open-ended questions. It can take us a while to master reflection, and that is okay. Many of us are not used to asking open-ended questions because yes/no questions come more naturally. Maybe you haven't really prioritized finding out what the caregiver thought during the support you provided because you understood EI to be about your work with the child. (That might be a hard pill to swallow but be honest with yourself. Remember, this is a judgment-free zone.) Or you might be great at self-reflection but trying to facilitate reflection with another person is another ball game (this can be true for me). Whatever the reason, be patient with yourself as you learn this skill. Pick a few open-ended questions that you like and work them into the conversation during each visit. Remember to pause to make space for the caregiver's answer. Resist the urge to fill up that space by answering the question yourself. Allow yourself to pause again as you process what you hear, then use that answer to guide intervention or ask for more information. To help you maintain the pause, take a slow deep breath, in and out, after asking your question, or count to 5 or 10 in your head, whatever works. Listen with a perspective of discovery, without assuming you know the answer. When the caregiver responds, be careful not to pass judgment on the reply. Instead, be grateful for the information and use it to think about your next steps.

Here is another important tip: It is absolutely okay to let the family know that you are learning a new skill. Explain the purpose of reflective conversation and let them know you would like to try it during your visit. Most caregivers will welcome the opportunity to help you grow too. If you need a refresher on reflective conversation, take another swing through Chapter 4.

Use "I wonder. . ." to prompt reflection and feedback. I love the phrase "I wonder. . ." because it can be both an effective prompt for reflection and a means to provide feedback. When used for reflection, you can wonder with the caregiver about why the child did or did not do something or why a strategy worked or didn't work. When sharing feedback, you can wonder what would happen if the caregiver tried a new strategy or tweaked a recently practiced strategy based on what you just observed. Wondering is a tool to help the caregiver consider the what, why, and how (EI Adult Learning Principle 3) of intervention. It is a gentle prompt to encourage the person you are wondering with to actively engage and think with you. Be careful, however, that you do not use wondering as a means of pushing your own agenda. Wonder with the caregiver and be open to ideas you may not have considered—ideas that come from tapping into that prior knowledge and experience the caregiver has with the child.

> "I wonder. . ." can be both an effective prompt for reflection and be a means to provide feedback.

Invite and share specific feedback. To reiterate the value that you place on the caregiver's active participation and input, invite him or her to provide feedback first. Questions such as, "How did that feel to you?" and "What did you think about that strategy?" can prompt the caregiver to reflect first before you provide feedback that could alter the caregiver's thinking. You can go deeper by asking for more specific feedback with questions such as, "What did you notice about how Amber reacted when you started the music?" or "What was different this time versus when you've tried this activity before?" This is clearly a reflective question, but in thinking about the answer, the caregiver will actually be giving him- or herself feedback. When it's your turn to provide feedback, be sure to think beyond the typical "Good job!" Describe what went well, such as, "I noticed that you used a soft voice to get Amber's attention when you tried to settle her down for her nap. That change in your voice really got her attention and cued her about what was coming next." Sometimes, you will have feedback that is more constructive, like when a strategy was not used successfully. In this case, it is especially important to start with the caregiver providing feedback first because caregivers usually know when something did not go as intended. When it is your turn, try to sandwich your feedback by providing one positive comment, one constructive comment, and another positive comment. Let's look at an example.

Pause

to PRACTICE   *Instructions:* Imagine that Amber's mother used her soft voice to call Amber to her and then started a tickle game that got Amber excited right before naptime. Read the example, circle the positive comments, and underline the constructive comment. Bonus point: Place a star above the reflective opportunity for Amber's mother.

> *"I really liked how you used a soft voice to prepare Amber for calming down. I know the tickle game is her favorite, but I think it might have excited her instead of calmed her down. What do you think? She loves being close to you so let's think of ways you can be together and help her calm herself before nap."*

To compare your answer to mine, visit page 167.

Lower your ego. Finally, facilitating caregiver practice, using reflective conversation, and providing specific feedback can require us, as professionals, to lower our egos a bit. Here's what I mean. We went to school for a long time to learn to do what we do. We know a ton about child development and EI. Yes, we could just "do" the intervention with the child much easier than teaching the caregiver to do it. When we lower our ego, we embrace our equal status with the caregiver. We both bring knowledge and experience to the visit, which will be most valuable when combined. Lowering your ego allows you to reflect and share feedback together, with equal importance placed on what is gained from this process. Lowering your ego also means sharing the responsibility for intervention. You do not bear it by yourself, nor does the caregiver. Instead, you bear the responsibility together as partners, practicing intervention during the visit, reflecting and sharing feedback reciprocally, and using what you both learn to purposefully plan for what happens between visits.

> You bear the responsibility for intervention together with the caregiver as partners, practicing intervention during the visit, reflecting and sharing feedback reciprocally, and using what you both learn to purposefully plan for what happens between visits.

Pause

and REFLECT   *Instructions:* Consider how you facilitate reflection and feedback during your visits. This requires an honest appraisal, especially if you have found these difficult to do. Ask yourself how comfortable you feel with reflection and feedback, why you feel that way, and what you need to feel more comfortable (if applicable). Describe how reflection and feedback were implemented on a recent visit. Because it can take a while to feel confident with reflection and feedback, try any new strategies you want to add to your practice for at least a month before you come back here to describe your experience.

My comfort level with facilitating reflection and feedback is:

_____ Not comfortable at all

_____ Somewhat comfortable

_____ Comfortable on most visits

Why?

_____

What I need to feel more comfortable:

_____

On a recent visit, I facilitated reflection and feedback by:

_____

_____

_____

When I facilitated reflection and feedback, I:

❏ Asked open-ended questions

❏ Used phrases like "I wonder. . ."

❏ Invited the caregiver's feedback and shared specific feedback with the caregiver

❏ Lowered my ego by embracing the caregiver as an equal partner

Action plan for using a new strategy:

_____

Experience using the strategy while facilitating balanced intervention:

_____

_____

Step 6: Planning for Between Visits

What happens between visits is far more important than what happens during visits; this can be a hard pill to swallow for our ego as well. Each visit seems like a pivotal moment in our week because of all that we do to prepare for, drive to, facilitate, and document it. For families, the visit is an hour among the 168 other hours during their busy week. It may be a particularly important hour for them, but if their focus, and ours, is primarily on what happens during that one hour, we miss our opportunity to enrich the child's experiences during the other 167.

Strategies for Between Visit Planning

Balance being present while focusing beyond the visit. This really is a mindful task to be thinking of both. As you get to know the family, store what you learn about their daily routines, activities, interests, and struggles in your memory. Refer to that information as you facilitate caregiver practice and reflection. Help the caregiver think about what she does in the moment, then expand her thinking to how she can use the same strategy after the visit, on another day, and during another routine. When you cannot practice in context during the visit, use your reflective conversation and information gathering to plan for strategy use outside of the visit (EI Adult Learning Principle 5). Always circle back on your next visit to find out if what was planned was successful and what else the caregiver needs to make it work between visits. This process, too, builds caregiver awareness, expands natural learning opportunities, and strengthens responsiveness and active participation.

> Help the caregiver think about what she does in the moment,
> then expand her thinking to how she can use the same strategy
> after the visit, on another day, during another routine.

Invite feedback on the visit. As you begin to wrap up the visit, take a moment to invite the caregiver's feedback by asking, "How do think today's visit went?" or "What did you think went well today?" This is an opportunity for you to learn from the caregiver. It also primes the caregiver for joint planning. In asking the caregiver to think out loud, you are encouraging active participation and reflection; both are essential to adult learning. After the caregiver has shared, feel free to share your thoughts too.

Review the visit and then let the caregiver decide. At the end of the visit, briefly review what you and the caregiver practiced and discussed. Ask the caregiver, "Based on what we did today, what would you like to try/keep working on between now and our next visit?" or "What strategy from today's visit would you like to keep using?" Let the caregiver pick a strategy and then work together to consider specifically how it will be used. Talk it out by asking, "When do you think you can practice that strategy?" and "What would that look like?" Help the caregiver think in specifics; this increases the likelihood that the strategy will be used and provides information for the written joint plan.

Write down the plan. As you can probably tell, I'm a big fan of a written joint plan. The plan should focus on something the caregiver identified as relevant and useful (EI Adult Learning Principle 1) and focus on action—how the caregiver and child will interact in a real context (EI Adult Learning Principles 4 and 5). When you write down the plan, be sure to include 1) a brief description of the strategy using simple, common language that everyone will understand; 2) the activity or routine the caregiver thinks will be useful; 3) how to use the strategy during that routine; and 4) why it is important or how the strategy will benefit the child's development or the family's quality of life. You can get all of this information from the joint planning discussion with the family. You can also invite the caregiver to write down the plan so it is in his or her own words, which can also make it easier to remember. Encourage the caregiver to post the written plan where it will be easily accessed, such as on the refrigerator. Some caregivers may prefer you to text or e-mail the plan so they have an electronic copy, so be sure to ask what works best for the family. Or, encourage the caregiver to take a photo of the joint plan to keep a copy stored on his or her phone. If you are working with a family for whom English is a second language, the interpreter can help translate the joint plan, write it down for the family, or help the family understand and record the plan in their own language.

Final tip: Be sure to leave the last 10 minutes of the visit for joint planning. Trying to come up with a joint plan in the final 2 minutes of a visit does not create the expectation that what the caregiver does with the child between visits is important. Don't rush the planning process; make it a priority to set the stage for what happens between visits.

Step 7: Wrap-Up and Scheduling

The wrap-up and scheduling process typically takes just a few additional minutes so be sure to leave time for that too.

Wrap-Up Strategies

Plan for what you will do during the next visit. After you've established the joint plan for between visits, it will be time to plan for what to do during the next visit. Again, let the caregiver choose. Use the IFSP outcomes as a guide and brainstorm together to determine what would be most helpful next time. Sometimes, caregivers know what they need help with or what they want you to observe, so planning for the next visit is easy. Other times, caregivers expect you to just come to the home and work with the child. Always ask the caregiver anyway. This reinforces the idea that you are there as a support and coach for the caregiver, not just as a therapist or specialist for the child. If the caregiver really does not have an idea, make a suggestion, perhaps based on information you gathered from the visit. For instance, maybe the caregiver shared earlier that his child was struggling with taking turns with older siblings. You might ask if it would be helpful for you to schedule the next visit later in the day when siblings are home so you can observe the tussle. As I've said before, make your suggestion but accept it gracefully if it is declined. Sometimes, you just have to go with the flow. Some visits will look different each time and others will look pretty similar week to week. Just do your best to offer opportunities for the caregiver to make decisions and access your support in ways that are most meaningful to the family.

Schedule the next visit. Based on the planning you just did, identify the date and time for the next visit. If you have the flexibility in your schedule, try to join the family at different times of day to see different interactions and routines. Or schedule around family priorities and needs. Many of us settle into a regular schedule, such as every Tuesday at 9 a.m., and this works well for families because it is predictable. Just don't forget that flexibility can be very beneficial too, especially when you want or need to join an activity that never happens on Tuesday at 9 a.m. After you have confirmed the next visit date and time, write it down, text it to the caregiver, or encourage the caregiver to add the visit to the family's paper or electronic calendar. Families of infants and toddlers have tons to remember so try to find a way to make it easier for them to keep up with your visits. You might also ask if the caregiver would like a reminder before the visit. Some caregivers find a simple call or text extremely helpful and others find it annoying, so be sure to ask.

Plan for between-visit check-ins and leave with gratitude. Decide together if the caregiver wants you to check in between visits. Or invite the caregiver to keep in touch by sending you a video or texting to let you know how strategy use goes. Periodic check-ins can be a great way to support what happens between visits, if the caregiver wants them. Keep in mind, however, that between-visit check-ins can occur at any time but you do not have to reply outside of business hours. Let the caregiver know that you monitor your e-mail, voicemail, and texts during business hours and you will respond as soon as you are back in the office. Welcome the updates but keep professional boundaries in mind.

Finally, as you leave, be sure to thank the caregiver for allowing you in the family's home (or wherever you meet). Leave with encouraging words and a genuine appreciation for the caregiver's and the child's effort. Celebrate what you saw during the visit and look forward to what comes next.

Pause

and REFLECT   *Instructions:* Combine Steps 6 and 7 because they both occur at the end of the visit. Think about a visit with a new family and a visit with a family you have known for 6 months or longer. Describe the process you typically use to plan with both caregivers and to wrap up the visits, noting if you use similar or different strategies depending on how long you have worked with a family.

For my visits with both families, I plan with the caregivers for between visits and wrap-up by:

_____

_____

When I plan for between visits and wrap-up with these families, I:

New	Experienced	
❏	❏	Balance being present with focusing on what happens between visits
❏	❏	Invite the caregiver's feedback about how the visit went
❏	❏	Review what we discussed and practiced with the caregiver
❏	❏	Let the caregiver decide what goes on the joint plan
❏	❏	Provide a written copy of the plan
❏	❏	Plan with the caregiver for what we will do next time
❏	❏	Schedule my next visit to accommodate our plan
❏	❏	Plan with the caregiver for between-visit check-ins (if helpful)
❏	❏	Leave with encouraging words and gratitude

If you notice a difference between how you plan and wrap up with new families versus families you have more experience supporting, think about possible reasons for the difference. Focus on your role and what you can do differently or better if you recognize a need to improve.

Action plan for using a new strategy:

_____

Experience using the strategy while facilitating balanced intervention:

_____

_____

ACHIEVING THE BALANCE

Anytime you read or learn about a new way to organize something you already do, you will (like caregivers in EI visits) compare it to what you already know and do. This is how you naturally balance new learning with prior knowledge and experience. As you completed the self-assessment and the pause and reflect activities, you were probably noticing which strategies rose to the top for you. Give yourself some time to integrate these practices into your daily work. To help you do this, I suggest that you take this book along in your car for the next week. Before and after each visit, reflect on the seven steps. Revisit your self-assessment frequently to see where you are making progress on using the strategies to balance your visits. Check in frequently with yourself about your intention and whether your practices are supporting the mission of EI. When you stumble, and you will, come back here to look for ideas you can use to pick yourself up. Achieving the balance between supporting caregiver and child learning is an intentional practice itself. Think about what you do and why and how you do it. Be an active participant in your own professional development. Reflect, seek feedback, and find support when you need it. Your learning does not stop here.

Pause

and REFLECT   *Instructions:* To illustrate the implementation of the seven steps, let's examine a scenario of an intervention visit. Read the scenario and pay attention to how the early interventionist, Evan, prepares for the visit, then uses the seven steps for conducting a balanced intervention visit. Note which strategies Evan uses too. You can refer to the self-assessment to refresh your memory.

Before his visit with Kiaan and his mother, Pari, Evan takes a few minutes at the office to prepare. He reviews his last contact note and the previous session's joint plan. He remembers that he will be observing Pari and Kiaan baking together because this is an activity they enjoy. While reviewing his note, Evan thinks about how he can help Pari address the IFSP outcome that focuses on Kiaan's ability to use two hands together in midline and to cross midline with either hand, which is hard for him due to his diagnosis of agenesis of corpus callosum. He considers bringing some playdough cutters, which might be fun to use in the dough, but decides not to so he can see what Pari and Kiaan naturally do instead. Evan sends a quick text to Pari to make sure she still wants to bake today. She quickly replies with a "thumbs up" and says she will see him soon.

During his drive to Pari's house, Evan gets a call from his wife, telling him their daughter is sick again with an earache. He is worried about her, but knows he needs to be fully present during his next visit. His wife says she will take their daughter to the pediatrician and text Evan after the appointment. Because they have a plan, Evan takes a deep breath and reorients himself to the visit as he pulls into the driveway. He rings the doorbell and is greeted by Kiaan at the door. Pari calls from the kitchen to tell him to come on in. He sees Kiaan's grandfather and older brother in the living room and stops to say hello. Once in the kitchen, Pari offers Evan an apron, which he puts on (even though it makes him feel a bit self-conscious). Evan asks about their week and specifically wonders how Kiaan did at the zoo, remembering that a family trip was planned for this past weekend. Pari said that Kiaan was able to walk in short bursts at the zoo while she held his hands the way Evan taught her (which was part of their previous joint plan). They celebrate this success while Pari puts Kiaan in his highchair at the end of the kitchen island. Evan asks Pari where he should stand, and she invites him to stand beside Kiaan.

Evan ask Pari about what they are baking and learns that she and Kiaan love to make his grandfather's favorite flat bread. Pari mixes the ingredients in a large bowl. Evan asks if Kiaan has ever helped stir the ingredients and Pari says no. He wonders if Kiaan might be able to practice crossing midline with the spoon while he stirs. Pari gives Kiaan the spoon and he immediately tries to lick it. Pari says that's why she has not let him stir before. Evan encourages her to help Kiaan learn to stir using hand-over-hand guidance. Pari tries and is surprised that after a few tries, Kiaan wants to stir on his own. Evan reflects with Pari about how stirring addresses Kiaan's IFSP outcome and provides feedback, telling Pari how he noticed that as soon as she felt Kiaan stirring, she eased her hand away so he could do it by himself. Pari says that she uses the same strategy often to teach Kiaan things.

Once the dough is mixed, Pari shows Evan and Kiaan how to knead it on the countertop. She puts a chunk in the middle of Kiaan's highchair tray and watches him. He does not grab for it right away so Pari takes his hand and touches the dough. He pulls his hand back and clearly does not want to touch the sticky dough. Pari says this is what typically happens, that Kiaan seems sensitive to how things feel. Evan asks Pari what she would like to see Kiaan do here so he can be sure he understands the problem. He can see that Kiaan is showing some tactile defensiveness, but he is not sure what Pari would like to do. Pari says she would like for Kiaan to knead the dough using both hands and maybe poke his fingers in, like with playdough. Evan and Pari brainstorm ideas for how to help Kiaan get more comfortable with the dough. Pari adds a bit more flour to the dough to make it less sticky and Kiaan seems more comfortable. They play together for a while, squishing the drier dough, poking it, and stacking dough balls.

Evan and Pari talk about how this activity could be used to encourage Kiaan to reach across midline and use his hands together. They come up with ideas to place the dough balls on the far right or left side of the tray so he must reach across his middle to get them. Pari isn't sure how to get Kiaan to reach across midline, so Evan asks if he can show her a strategy that he thinks might work. He explains that he will gently block Kiaan's hand (the one on the same side as the balls) while counting with Kiaan as he reaches across the tray to pick up a ball with his other hand. He suggests they have a cup handy for Kiaan to drop the ball into. They place the dough balls on the left side of the tray. Evan models the strategy by blocking Kiaan's left hand so he has to use his right hand to pick up the balls. He also counts 1-2-3 as Kiaan picks up a ball and drops it into the cup. They cheer when Kiaan is successful. Evan asks Pari what she noticed, and she replies that she liked how the counting distracted Kiaan. She also saw how Evan blocked Kiaan's left hand by touching his wrist instead of holding his whole hand, which he probably would not have liked. Evan asks if Pari wants to try and she says yes. She tries the same strategies with Kiaan several times. Evan coaches Pari when she needs support with helping Kiaan use the correct hand. After the practice, Evan reflects with Pari and invites her feedback. He asks, "How did that feel to you?" and "How could you use these same strategies during other parts of the day?" They discuss other routines, such as getting Kiaan to hand Pari his shoes when they get ready to go outside by offering each shoe to Kiaan on the opposite sides so he has to reach across his midline to get them. Evan likes that idea and wonders with Pari if she might also be able to use the counting technique while she helps him walk. When Kiaan is ready to get out of the highchair, they practice helping him walk with support and use counting to encourage him to take extra steps.

At the end of the visit, Evan asks Pari how she thinks the visit went. He also asks her what strategy she would like to try using with Kiaan before the next visit. Pari decides to use the counting strategy when they practice walking and use the hand blocking strategy whenever she sees an opportunity, such as during bath time or snack times. Evan writes out the joint plan and Pari takes a photo of the plan with her phone. Then, they discuss what to do next time. Pari says she would like more ideas to help Kiaan with his walking, so maybe they can spend time in the backyard if the weather is nice. Evan thinks that is a great idea and wonders if they could also try getting Kiaan to use his hands in his brother's sandbox. Pari says that she is not sure Kiaan will want to touch the sand, but she is willing to give it a try. They schedule the next visit for a morning time slot because that is when the children typically play outside. Evan confirms with Pari that he will text her before the next visit to check in. He leaves the visit by giving Kiaan a "fist bump" for his great work today and thanks Pari and her father for inviting him to their home.

1. Which steps and strategies did Evan use during this visit? Use the self-assessment to guide your answers.

2. What feedback would you give Evan?

3. How does Evan's visit compare to how you conduct visits? What did he do that you liked?

Evan's visit provides a shining example of how to use these steps and strategies. You might be thinking that the families you support are not typically engaged as Pari was. Or, perhaps you work supporting families with children with more complex needs. If you are feeling any resistance to this scenario or using the steps or strategies, journal about it to investigate your feelings. Try not to let resistance block your progress. No approach to conducting EI visits will be perfect, just as there is no perfect visit. Grant yourself the flexibility to ease into using these strategies and the grace to struggle. Struggle is essential to growth, so welcome it.

In the end, I hope you find that the strategies in this chapter, and in Chapter 4, add some tools to your intervention toolbox. How you use your tools will look different from visit to visit, and family to family. The key is to keep up your commitment to evolving your practices. It will be so easy, I promise you, to slip back into old practices, especially when implementing new ones and seeking balance becomes difficult. Commitment, focus, and persistence are so important in this work, but so is self-care. Our last chapter will conclude this book with an emphasis on how to take good care of yourself as an early interventionist.

With so much to learn, so many children and families to see, so many regulations to keep up with, so much paperwork, and so many miles to drive, it is often difficult for us to take care of ourselves. Just as I said before—that there is no team without the family—there is also no EI team without you. Families need you to be the best you can be. Your program needs the same thing. Your own family needs you too. Let's shift gears to think about how to manage your workload, soothe your stress, continue your learning, and seek support from others so that you can be present, mindful, and healthy doing the work you love.

> "
> THERE COMES A MOMENT IN EVERY LIFE WHEN THE UNIVERSE PRESENTS YOU WITH AN OPPORTUNITY TO RISE TO YOUR POTENTIAL. AN OPEN DOOR THAT ONLY REQUIRES THE HEART TO WALK THROUGH, SEIZE IT AND HANG ON. THE CHOICE IS NEVER SIMPLE. IT'S NEVER EASY. IT'S NOT SUPPOSED TO BE. BUT THOSE WHO TRAVEL THIS PATH HAVE ALWAYS LOOKED BACK AND REALIZED THAT THE TEST WAS ALWAYS ABOUT THE HEART. . . . THE REST IS JUST PRACTICE.
> "
>
> —Jaime Buckley

CHAPTER 5

Reflective Journal

Instructions: Use this space to capture your thoughts about what you learned in Chapter 5.

NEW IDEAS: _____

_____

_____

_____

_____

_____

_____

IDEAS THAT CHALLENGED ME: _____

_____

_____

_____

_____

_____

_____

THOUGHTS & FEELINGS: _____

_____

_____

_____

_____

_____

_____

Action Plan

Instructions: Based on your reflections and the self-assessment in this chapter, what do you want to do next? Continue your commitment to yourself with another action plan. Be sure to check in with yourself periodically to see if you are following the intention you set here. If not, review the chapter and make a new plan. Remember, your commitment and persistence are key.

By _____ (date),

I will intentionally use balanced intervention practices that facilitate learning for caregivers and

children during visits by _____

_____ (action).

> (action examples: emphasizing that EI visits are practice sessions for the caregiver and child, using observation more frequently to help me understand family routines, using modeling as a teaching tool, sharing specific feedback, writing down the joint plan)

ACTION PLAN COMPLETED ☐

My key takeaway: _____

_____

_____

TIPS:
- Identify several families with whom you can track your progress on using the steps and strategies. Make multiple copies of the self-assessment, label them with a number for each family, and keep them with you. Complete an initial self-assessment for your work with each family and then complete the self-assessment again after several visits. Reflect on the practices and strategies you used after each visit over the course of a month or two. Give yourself time to see progress, but make sure you are reflecting regularly so you stay in tune with your intention to integrate specific practices.

- Use the content in this chapter to host a lunch and learn meeting in your program. Invite your colleagues to complete the self-assessment before the meeting and then discuss insights and plans for improvement at the meeting. Share information about each of the seven steps and then brainstorm with your colleagues about using the strategies or adding any that they have found useful. Problem-solve together to support anyone who is struggling to balance intervention with a family.

- Using what you learned in this chapter, compare the practices you use during your easiest visit and your most challenging visit. Process this with a colleague or your supervisor and problem-solve together to find ways to use the seven steps and strategies to make that challenging visit feel more successful.

- Pull together a community of practice with your colleagues to really think about how to use the information in this chapter (or the whole book). Meet regularly to process each of the seven steps (or each chapter) and support each other in evolving your practices so that the intervention support you provide becomes more balanced and effective.

"

BE THERE FOR OTHERS,
BUT NEVER LEAVE
YOURSELF BEHIND.

"

—Dodinsky

6

Taking Care of Yourself

Close your eyes and take a deep, cleansing breath. Focus on yourself and how you feel right now. Maybe you've had a busy day of hopping from one visit to the next. Maybe you are squeezing in some reflection between visits, parked outside of a convenience store or sitting in a coffee shop. Or, perhaps you are reading at breakfast before your day begins. Wherever you are, pause and think about the work you've done here in this book. You have focused on how to deepen your EI practices so that you can be there for families, supporting the active participation and learning of both caregivers and children. You've already done a lot of work for others; your commitment to this book speaks to that. Now it's time to think about what you can do for yourself.

WHERE DO YOU FIT IN?

Believe me, I get it. I know how hard it can be to find time to take care of yourself in the midst of a career as an early interventionist. We tend to prioritize our work and the families we see over our own self-care. We push through visit after visit, taking only moments to eat lunch or go to the bathroom. We work hard to be on time to visits and be present for families, while forgetting to show up for ourselves and give ourselves time to process what we experience, time to breathe in calmness and breathe out the stress of the day. Many of us serve high numbers of families. Some of us only get paid per visit so we squeeze in as many as six to eight visits a day and then write our contact notes in the evenings instead of resting or recharging. We dream about families at night, worrying about children who are in situations that haunt us. We use our time between visits to call our colleagues for teaming, to celebrate a milestone, or to process a challenge. Working as an EI service provider can be strenuous and isolating, so it is vitally important that you take time to fit yourself into your day. This chapter will focus on you and how to make space for self-care and self-management skills so that you have the time and energy you need to be present for families. You are just as important as any child or family you see. Don't forget where you fit in, because you matter too.

Pause
and REFLECT

Instructions: This final self-assessment will help you reflect on what you do now to manage your workload and take care of yourself. You may be tempted to skip it, but think about this: Skipping this is like skipping over yourself. Give yourself the next few minutes to focus on what you do and what you need. You won't regret it.

Self-Assessment: Taking Care of Yourself and Managing Your Workload

	Never	Not Very Often	Sometimes	Most of the Time	Always	Notes to Explain My Answers
I prioritize 20 minutes each day to relax and recharge.						
I have an organizational system in place to keep track of my work.						
I maintain work boundaries that separate work from my personal life.						
I am able to keep up with completing my required documentation.						
I am on time to visits with families.						
I intentionally plan for space in my day for completing my documentation.						
I prioritize my own learning so I can evolve my practices.						
I plan for travel time between visits with enough cushion that I am not rushed from one place to the next.						

	Never	Not Very Often	Sometimes	Most of the Time	Always	Notes to Explain My Answers
I have people I can talk to when I need to process how I feel or what I experience.						
I am intentional about managing my work stress.						
I reach out to my support system when I need them.						
I regularly participate in professional development to keep my knowledge and skills current.						
I take on only as much as I can truly manage without excessive stress.						
I schedule my day so that I flow through it with time and space to take care of my needs as well as the needs of families.						
At the end of the day, I feel like what I did was important.						

Read back over your self-assessment and notice where most of your answers fall. Are they more in the Never or Not very often columns? If yes, then working through this chapter will be especially important because you are probably so busy that you are not prioritizing yourself in your day. I know, it's hard when expectations are high, you have to get paid, and there is never enough of you to go around. Think of yourself as a cup. If your cup is empty, then you will not have anything left to fill up another's cup. You can't give what you don't have, so now is your time to examine how you spend your day. It can feel impossible, but even one or two good self-care or self-management strategies fit into your day can make a world of difference.

If you found your answers to be squarely in the Sometimes column, my guess is that you are busy but trying hard to manage. This can be true of answers that bounce around between Never and Always too. If your answers leaned toward the right and were mostly in the Most of the time or Always columns, stick with me because you are someone who prioritizes self-care in your work so you are probably open to learning another good strategy.

Or, of course, you could put this book down and go hang out with yourself for a while, but I encourage you to keep doing what you do well. Keep taking care of yourself by reading this last chapter. Wherever you are on the continuum, openness to examining your practices—especially those that focus on *you*—is valuable and time well spent.

> Openness to examining your practices—especially those that
> focus on *you*—is valuable and time well spent.

A JUDGMENT-FREE ZONE

I find that reflecting on your professional practices with families is often easier that reflecting on your self-care or how you organize and manage yourself. Perhaps this is because your practices with families can seem like they are "outside" of yourself or even bigger than you, when in fact they are quite personal. Reflecting on and assessing your personal practices, those you use to manage your time, complete your documentation, and take care of yourself, can feel very personal, be easily judged, and be placed low on the priority list. What I mean here is that you will hear EI practitioners say things like, "I'm terrible at time management but I love my families" or "Taking care of myself during the day just isn't as important as getting my work done." I encourage you to approach this chapter as another judgment-free zone. When you hear thoughts like these creeping in, take a deep breath and breathe them out. Either replace them with a positive statement like, "I matter too" or "Taking time for myself will make me more effective with families." Whether you do or do not already use the strategies we'll discuss is neutral, no judgment. Be kind to yourself and be on the lookout for a strategy or two that will help you have more ease in your day.

TIME MANAGEMENT STRATEGIES

Time management is essential to your healthy survival as an EI practitioner, whether you are a service coordinator or a service provider. Some of us enter into this complex field with our planners ready and our built-in time management systems primed; others are blind-sided with all of the responsibilities, timelines, and places to be. Even with planners ready and calendar apps downloaded, I think it takes time to learn how to manage your time effectively in this field. By effectively, I mean finding your own system that ensures that you get your work done in a timely manner with as little stress as possible. Here are some strategies for scheduling intervention visits, breaks, travel time, and time for documentation to consider adding to your system.

Scheduling Intervention Visits

Cluster visits in the same area. When you schedule your days, be as intentional as you can to schedule visits in the same area on the same day. This can be challenging when you try to accommodate family schedules and practice flexibility to join family routines and activities, but try to cluster your visits to minimize your travel time to and from any areas, especially those that are far away. There is a caveat to this strategy: Choosing to cluster our visits cannot mean that you tell families you are only in their area on Tuesdays. Clustering is a great strategy when families have flexibility; when family schedules are less flexible or the routine you need to observe happens on a different day, clustering may not work. Use it when you can but remain flexible.

Block one full hour on your calendar for 45-minute visits. This tip is all about perspective. It's similar to the strategy people use to avoid being late when they set their clocks back 10 minutes. If you schedule 45-minute visits, block 1 hour on your schedule so you have a cushion in case the family needs a little more time. You can also use this time to jot down notes about the visit that you can use when you type up your contact note later. Or this time can be used to contact other team members from your car between visits. Or, maybe that extra 15 minutes will ensure that you have some breathing room, a quick potty break, or a moment to read this book on your lunch break.

Make being on time a priority. When you are on time for visits, you show respect for the family's time. When you are consistently late, whether you call or text the family a heads-up, you are not showing respect and it can be perceived as less professional, especially if you show up frazzled at being late. Check in with yourself about your beliefs about being on time. If you approach your arrival time as flexible and expect the family to understand, then think about how you feel when you visit doctors or schedule a plumber and they are always running late. It's frustrating and can color your interactions with that person, even if you understand the reason for the lateness. Give yourself the space in your schedule to ensure that you will be on time. In my area, we have lots of waterways and drawbridges that lift on the hour. To go anywhere on time, I have to be mindful of bridge lifts and leave early enough in case I get caught by one. Sure, families would understand because they live here too, but it is not the family's responsibility to accommodate me. When I was providing direct services, I knew it was my job to accommodate them. That included planning my day so that I would be on time.

Be realistic with your daily load. It can be so tempting to agree to squeeze one more visit in. Who really needs a lunch break anyway? You do! Figure out how many visits you can do in a day and remain sane, healthy, and energized. Some of you will have daily targets set by your agency for direct service hours. Usually, you have control over how these hours are scheduled. Reach your targets but be realistic about how many visits you can manage back to back.

Scheduling Breaks

Block time for breaks. This is a strategy that I'll admit I struggle with. I can almost always find a reason to avoid a break. There is always more work to do or another e-mail to send. Try to be intentional about scheduling yourself a morning, lunch, and afternoon break. Or at least find time for two out of the three. Shoot for breaks of at least 15–20 minutes and start smaller if you need to. Scheduling time for yourself is a healthy habit that helps you recharge and remain in that mental space where you are ready to follow the family's lead and have the energy you need to engage both the caregiver and the child.

Schedule time to move. Consider scheduling at least 15–20 minutes for a movement break during your day. That may seem like a luxury, I know, but scheduling time to move can help you break up all of the sitting you inevitably do while traveling and engaging families. Hopefully, after reading this book, you'll find yourself sitting on the floor less because you'll be moving about with the family more. Even so, we sit a lot in EI. Taking a walk in a park or a spin around the mall can be a wonderful reset button. If you like, set a step goal for your day and seek out interesting ways to reach it. Take the stairs when working in apartment buildings. Park your car at the end of the lot or around the corner from the home you are visiting (as long as it's safe to do so). These brief walks can be breaks too.

Call a friend. To help you actually take your break, consider calling a friend for 10 minutes. That can help your mind reset and can energize you too. If possible, avoid talking about work because if you spend your break talking about, e-mailing about, or online searching about work, it's not really a break, is it?

Schedule time to do nothing. Wow, even typing that in this book is hard for me. Doing "nothing" is not one of my superpowers but I hope it will be one of yours. Dedicate time to just sit, breathe, look around, listen to the birds or the rain, and empty your mind. You might choose to spend this time meditating, which is not really doing nothing, I know. Meditation is an evidence-based way to clear your mind and is a skill that you can learn with practice. It is calming, centering, and can be accomplished in 10 minutes a day before work, while parked in your car between visits, or at the end of your busy day.

Pause
to RECHARGE

Instructions: Read the instructions below to help you settle into meditation for 10 minutes. Consider recording yourself reading the guided meditation that follows, and then play the recording back and listen as you settle in. Commit to yourself that you will stay still and quiet for 10 minutes or work up to 10 minutes over a week or so, meditating 1 minute longer each time. When you are finished, come back here and jot down how you feel.

Find a quiet, comfortable seat—in your car, on a blanket at the park, or in your office with the door closed. Uncross your ankles and place your hands palms-up on your thighs or knees. Close your eyes and take deep, slow breaths. Tune your attention into your breathing to follow your inhales and exhales. When your mind wanders and thoughts take over, notice them and let them go. Let them float away while you come back to your breath. It's very common for your thoughts to take over, especially during the workday. Just notice them and then resettle your attention on your breath, in and out. This back and forth is very normal as you get accustomed to meditation. Continue tuning into your breath for 10 minutes. When it is time to come out of your meditation, take a long, deep breath in through your nose and out through your mouth. Gently wiggle your hands and feet, or stretch. Slowly open your eyes and sit a few seconds more. Try not to jump right back on your phone or into work. Sit with how you feel, and then come back here and capture your feelings in writing.

After meditation, I feel:

_____

_____

Note: If you would like help with learning to meditate during your breaks, look for guided meditation apps or videos online.

Scheduling Travel Time

Intentionally block travel time in your schedule. This may seem like a no-brainer but recording your travel time in your planner can help you see how much time you actually spend in transit. It can also give you a visual reminder about the importance of scheduling enough time (or more than enough) to be sure you will be on time to your next visit.

Plan for a cushion. Calculate how long it takes between visits and add 10–15 extra minutes to give you a cushion should you run into a traffic snarl, get caught at train tracks, or find yourself slowed down by an errant cow in the road (true story). This also helps reduce your stress level should your previous visit run long. If you know that a visit always runs over the time you had planned, then planning for a cushion is especially important.

Use travel time to recharge. Rather than rushing from visit to visit, be intentional about how to spend this time so that you recharge rather than carry stress from one setting to the next, especially when you have challenging visits. Listen to a podcast or an audiobook. Practice deep breathing and mindful attention to what you see, hear, and feel. Or just roll down your window and clear your mind.

> Rather than rushing from visit to visit, be intentional about how to spend this time so that you recharge rather than carry stress from one setting to the next.

Scheduling Time for Documentation

Documentation is the beast of EI. Most programs have documentation requirements tied to billing, family rights and procedural safeguards, and local, state, and federal policies and procedures. Managing your documentation skillfully is similar to managing your time—you may have been pre-programmed to do this well or you may struggle to keep up. Try these strategies if you are looking for a way to improve this part of your work.

Record shorthand notes or voice memos after each visit. I know, it's not always possible to write your contact note during or immediately after each visit. After you get back in your car, take 2–3 minutes to record notes about how the IFSP outcomes were addressed, including the routines or activities that occurred during the visit and what each participant did, how the caregiver and child interacted, what intervention strategies were practiced, and so forth. Note any progress or challenges and be sure to capture the joint plan. You can refer to these notes or the voice memo later when you have time to write the complete contact note. Whichever format you use to capture these abbreviated notes, be sure to protect child and family confidentiality; it's probably best to avoid recording the family's names or other identifying information. Use initials or refer to the date and time of the visit so you can identify which note goes with which visit later, when it is time to write the contact note.

Block time at the end of the day or one afternoon each week. Several service coordinators I know will block the last hour of each day to catch up on documentation. I have also heard suggestions for blocking one day or one afternoon each week to make sure documentation is current. Some practitioners avoid scheduling visits on Fridays so they can end their week with all documentation in order. Choose the option that fits your style and your schedule, but do so with intention. Block this time weekly for the next several months and do your best not to schedule something else during this window. Consider it sacred time.

Pause
and REFLECT   *Instructions:* Using the following table, consider what strategies you already use and what strategies you would like to use to manage your schedule. Pay attention to each of the four areas discussed here: scheduling intervention visits, breaks, travel time, and documentation.

	Scheduling intervention visits	Scheduling travel time	Scheduling breaks (Don't skip this one!)	Scheduling time for documentation
Strategies I already use				
Strategies I will add to my practice				

STRATEGIES FOR COMPLETING DOCUMENTATION

Scheduling the time to complete the required documentation is one important step; completing it accurately is another. You probably have state and local requirements for required forms, required components to your contact notes, and required timelines for entering documentation into your record system. Here are some strategies for managing those documentation requirements so that they don't suck the life right out of you.

Prepare as much as possible. Before an assessment or IFSP meeting, prep your documentation as much as you can. Fill out the child's demographics and determine adjusted age (if the child was a preemie) on your assessment protocols before you leave the office. Prepare demographics and write or type out whatever you already know about the child and family on the IFSP before the meeting. For instance, if the intake was thorough, you probably have information about the family's daily routine, their priorities, resources, and concerns, as well as information about the child's referral and medical history. Add these to the plan early so that you can focus on gathering new information for the IFSP in the meeting. However, you should never type the IFSP outcomes onto the form before the IFSP meeting because outcomes should be written with the family. You may think you know what the outcomes "should" be, but be careful to avoid presumptions. Outcomes belong to the family; same with the services. Never pre-populate that part of the plan, either. If you are the service coordinator who will review procedural safeguards or transition referral forms, prepare as much of these in advance as possible. This will make any meeting with the family go more smoothly and show the family that you are prepared and ready to focus on them. Plus, going into a meeting prepared will also make you feel better.

Use a system to keep you organized. Pause now and think about how you keep up with your documentation. Are you winging it and barely remembering what to do for whom? Or are you organized, even if you get a little behind sometimes? Or, perhaps you've got it down to a science. Wherever you are, try to articulate your organization system here.

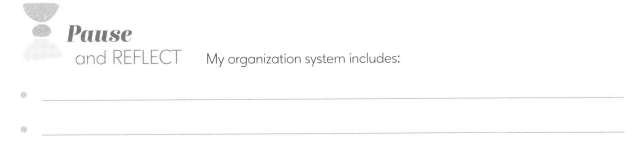

Pause
and REFLECT   My organization system includes:

_____

_____

_____

For me, I used to do lists to keep me organized. I would include a check box beside each intervention visit in my schedule that I would check when the contact note was written and filed or uploaded. I also had a spreadsheet with information about all of the families I supported that included all activities along the EI process (initial evaluation and assessment, initial IFSP, 6-month IFSP reviews, transition referral) and required timelines. Posting this list where I could see it and refer to it daily helped me ensure that timelines were met and families received the services they were entitled to in a timely fashion. I also used this spreadsheet in supervision when updating my supervisor about my work.

Set reminders. Use your tools. If your program uses an electronic medical record system, use notifications or flags to make sure you don't miss timelines. Set reminders in your calendar for when IFSP reviews are due, when you need to contact families or other team members, and when you need to have your documentation in the record (many programs require contact notes to be in the child's record within 2–5 days from the date of service). Here's another important tip: Set these reminders to give yourself some room to accomplish the tasks. Don't set the IFSP review reminder for the actual date the child's IFSP expires; instead, set the reminder a month or two ahead of time so you can contact team members, schedule the review, and prepare the documentation. Use electronic reminders to help you prioritize time to take a break in your day too. I literally have to schedule reminders to take breaks because without them, I just keep working and forget to rest. If that sounds like you, then use your tools to help you do what's required and prioritize what you need.

Approach documentation like every file could be audited at any time. Yes, this is the greatest anxiety trigger in the EI world: the dreaded record audit, when your supervisor, a peer, or a quality assurance (QA) monitor reviews a child's record for which you are responsible. Rather than scrambling to clean up your records before that quarterly or annual audit, try to approach managing each record as if it could be audited at any time. I used to think about my records this way—it is a parent's right to see his or her child's record at any time. I wanted the records I managed to be well-organized and complete in case this happened. That way, if one of my files was spontaneously pulled for audit, I didn't have to sweat it. I knew the contents were current. Sure, I still slipped up occasionally, but I stacked the deck in my favor by always viewing my records from an audit perspective.

Audit yourself on a regular basis. With that in mind, block time to periodically audit yourself. If possible, get a copy of the form your supervisor or QA officer uses to audit records and take a swing through the records you are responsible for. Block time to audit a certain number of your records each month. That way, you can catch errors and fix them before someone else finds them. (This is a great tip for service coordinators.) For example, did you know that if even one record is out of compliance on the 45-day timeline between the initial referral and the date the caregiver signs the IFSP, then your program is out of compliance and your state will be out of compliance too? That's a heady thing to realize, especially if you are a service coordinator. The 45-day timeline is a federal requirement and compliance is set at 100%. Now, imagine that for one family, the child became ill so the family needed to postpone the initial IFSP meeting. If this is documented in the child's record, then you, your program, and your state are not considered out of compliance. If, however, you forget to document the family's scheduling preference, then all of you are out of compliance. You know the saying: if it's not documented, it didn't happen. Make sure that you document what did happen thoroughly and you will be fine.

Keep a checklist of required documentation or required components for each child's record. If your program does not have this, make it for yourself. Make a list of all of the required forms for all of the activities along the EI process. Similarly, make a list of all requirements for each child's record. Use these lists when setting up a new record or when processing a child and family into your program. Check things off as you complete them, and periodically review your checklists to make sure everything is complete. You probably know the required forms like the back of your hand but using checklists can take some of the cognitive load off of you. You don't have to mentally store things like this when you can externally store them in writing or electronically. If you are not a service coordinator, you might be thinking that this is less relevant for you because perhaps you don't actually manage the child's record. It's good practice, however, for all professional team members to know what documentation is required because even though you might not be responsible for managing the file, your signature is still often required on important documentation. Therefore, it is important to be sure you know what you're signing and what is required.

Ask others for tips and advice. Several of these tips so far require checklists or systems. Rather than creating one from scratch, always ask around first. Chances are that your colleagues already have checklists, spreadsheets, or systems they use that they will be willing to share. In fact, EI practitioners tend to love sharing what works for them. Ask around, take advice, and adapt what you find to fit your style.

Pause
and REFLECT   *Instructions:* Pick a strategy for completing documentation to either add to your practices or share with your colleagues by e-mail, text, or in your next staff meeting.

Strategy I will use or share: _____

_____

STRATEGIES FOR STRESS MANAGEMENT

For some of us, just thinking about an organizational system or completing documentation raises our cortisol levels. For others, our sources of stress tend to be more emotional, like worrying about how we can help an under-resourced family. Sometimes, interactions between team members can be stressful, especially when we have different values or beliefs about how to support families, get our work done, or collaborate. Supporting lots of families or a smaller number of families with high needs, having extensive driving time from visit to visit, or juggling multiple roles (e.g., one person who is a supervisor, service provider, and service coordinator) can also be ongoing sources of stress. I once heard someone say that stress is all about perspective. An event is stressful because you perceive it that way. I try hard to remember that, but sometimes I feel the stress deep in my body, almost before my mind perceives it. However you process stress and whatever your triggers are, try these strategies to help you manage.

Listen and observe. Listen to your body. Observe how you move and how you feel through the day. If you are tied up in knots, feeling hurried or frustrated or depleted, then it is probably a good time to take a deep breath and evaluate the situation. This is especially important because we can get in a habit of living stressfully as EI practitioners. Try this exercise to observe yourself and see how you are.

Pause
and REFLECT   *Instructions:* Pause for a few moments, close your eyes, listen and observe your body. Notice where you feel tension. Observe your thoughts to find out what you are ruminating about right now. Record what you observe here.

Where I am feeling tension: _____

What I'm thinking about: _____

At this moment, my stress level is:

Low   Medium   High

Why? _____

I can help myself right now by: _____

Consider what you would tell a friend or colleague who filled out this activity as you did. What advice would you give? How might you suggest that person nurture him- or herself? Now, take your own advice.

Take 20 minutes for yourself every day. Find at least 20 minutes each day to do something for yourself, to downshift or re-center. What these 20 minutes looks like will be completely up to you and may differ day to day. Use this time to exercise, read a book, listen to music or a podcast, write in your journal, walk or play with your dog, relax in your hammock (my personal favorite), meditate, take a bath, snuggle with your kids, work on a puzzle, drink a cup of tea, knit, call a friend, or simply do nothing at all. Figure out what recharges your soul and make time for it every day.

> Figure out what recharges your soul and make time for it every day.

Process your work experiences with colleagues (not families). Sometimes, the best medicine for work stress is to talk with someone who understands. Share how you feel and process your experiences with a trusted colleague or supervisor. Vent if you need to (because we all do at times) but do so respectfully. Support others who are stressed, which can make you feel better too. Just remember to avoid sharing your stressors with families. They will often care deeply about you and may even ask how you are. Be mindful of professional boundaries, sharing only as much as necessary. Never talk about personal stressors with families and do not vent to them. They deserve your best face forward. If you find that you cannot give that to them, then talk to your supervisor, reschedule the visit, or consider if you are the right person to partner with that family.

Be mindful of your attitude and how you think. When you're stressed, it can be easy to let it eat away at your attitude, sometimes without even realizing it. Remember earlier when we talked about taking responsibility for the energy you bring into the room? Well, the same principle applies to the energy you bring to work. If you are burned out, negative about families, or exasperated about work responsibilities, you can spread that to your colleagues. Strong feelings like these leech off of us and become contagious if we are not careful. Instead, catch yourself, reflect, take a break when you need it, and decide to be a source of positive energy in your office. Sure, you will have your down days, but just be mindful to not let them take over. If they do, talk with someone you trust to help you manage your feelings and consider your options.

> When you are feeling stressed, catch yourself, reflect, take a break when you
> need it, and decide to be a source of positive energy in your office.

If you find yourself frustrated or angry about a family situation, check in with yourself about what you are thinking. Reframe negative perceptions or thoughts in a more positive light (rather than "Jaqui's mother keeps canceling our visits. She doesn't care what we're doing" to "I'm doing my best to engage Jaqui's mother. Maybe she has other important things going on. I'm going to talk to my colleague for new ideas"). Consider that what your brain tells you is not always correct or even true (Amen, 2015). That was an epiphany for me to learn. It's okay to question your thoughts, disregard ones that don't serve you, and replace them with ideas that are more accurate, truthful, and helpful. When you notice that your attitude about a family or a certain situation has soured, acknowledge where you are and do whatever helps you reset.

Stay organized. We've already discussed organization strategies so I won't add more here. Suffice it to say that the more organized you are, the more likely that you will feel better about your workload and less stressed about managing it. Just don't overthink it. If you end up worrying for an hour about how to properly color-code that Excel spreadsheet, then you might want to back away from your computer and take a nice, long brain break.

Say "no." This is a hard one. Many of us in EI are people pleasers and helpers. We say "yes" when we can help someone else, forgetting to say "no" when it does not serve our own self-care. If you are like me, you may tend to say "yes!" before you even think about it. There will be times when you cannot say "no" to a job responsibility, but before you agree to take on another task, at least pause. It is almost always okay to ask for some time to think about your response. You may not be able to say "no" to that new referral, but you can certainly talk with your supervisor about feeling overwhelmed before you say "yes" or ask the service coordinator for some time to think about it so you can consider your current workload. Just check in with yourself before you take on more work, whenever you can.

Set boundaries and leave it at work. Okay, full disclosure: This one is also a struggle for me. Leaving work at work and not taking it home can be hard in this profession. We care deeply about our families and sometimes bring home our emotions, tension, or exhaustion. If you find yourself thinking about families a lot when you are not at work, dreaming about them, or even taking their calls outside of work hours, it is definitely time for a self-check. If you find yourself talking a lot about work (okay, complaining) at home, again, press pause and do some self-examination.

When work is leaking into or negatively affecting your personal life, it's time to check your boundaries. If you notice your boundaries between work and home are slipping, shore up those walls and reestablish them. Boundaries are so important because they allow you to be present where you are—present at work because you have separated your personal and professional lives and present at home with your family and friends because you have left work at work. Sounds easy, right? I know it's not easy; it takes intention, attention, and action. Add physical cues to your day to help you recognize your boundaries. Wait to put your badge or nametag on until you get to your office and take it off at the end of the day before you go home. Develop a transition routine between home and work, such as listening to a radio show or audiobook that you only treat yourself to during this time. Use 4×4 breathing (breathe in for 4 seconds, hold for 4 seconds, breathe out for 4, pause for 4, repeat) in the car to get yourself centered before you enter your home at the end of the day. Close your eyes and imagine your work day running off of you like river water pouring over a boulder. I work from home so my boundaries can get very thin. I purposefully close my window shades, turn off my lights, clean up my desk space, and push in my chair to signal to myself that my work day is over. I am able to check my work e-mail on my smartphone but I have the app hidden so it is not on my phone's homescreen. I have to go looking for it and I have the notifications turned off—that way, I am less tempted to check my work e-mail outside of work hours. When I keep to my boundaries, I'm happier and better balanced. I think you will be too.

> Close your eyes and imagine your work day running off
> of you like river water pouring over a boulder.

Ask for help when you need it. There is no weakness in asking for help. You help families all day; it is absolutely okay to need help yourself. If you are feeling stressed, schedule time to talk with your supervisor. Before that meeting, however, consider how you're feeling and what words best reflect your experience, and try to come up with an idea or two for improving your situation. Your supervisor may be more likely to work with you when you present possible solutions to a problem. Perhaps you need a pause on new referrals for a week to catch up. Maybe taking some time off would help. Ask for the help you need and access the support network you have. If you find that you need more help than your network can provide, ask for more formalized help. Seeking out counseling can be one of the best things you can do for yourself.

Take a day off. What? Take a day off? Are you crazy? I have 25 children to see each week and paperwork to do and. . . Okay, breathe. If you laughed when you saw this suggestion or any of the thoughts you just read actually did run through your mind, it's probably time to take a day off. Take a mental health day. Take a day for you. If a whole day seems impossible, take an afternoon off. If you have leave time through your employer, use it.

Take a vacation. Okay, now we're getting crazy here. A whole week off? Yes! Take a vacation or even a staycation. You may love your work, but time away can be just what you need to balance your life and refresh yourself. Pick the week far in advance so you can plan for how you will make up visits and manage your responsibilities. Prepare for your vacation so you can leave work behind and focus on relaxation, fun, connection with your family, or whatever you look forward to during that time. Just remember, when you take time off, that means time off—no work-related e-mails, phone calls, or squeezing in a meeting here or there. Time. Off.

Find your balance. You love what you do, so why does it matter to take time off or pay attention to your stress? When we get rooted in a stressful work life, we can get so accustomed to it that we fail to even notice it, leading to an imbalance. More of our energy is sapped in the work stress we feel so we have less energy for the rest of our life, for our families, and for ourselves. In the Pause and Reflect that follows, take a moment to consider how this plays out in your work–life balance.

Pause and REFLECT

Instructions: Think about your life over the course of 1 week. Use the circle below to visualize where your energy goes by making a pie chart. If you find that you are out of balance, yielding too much energy to work, then jot down some ideas for how to regain your balance and set a goal for yourself.

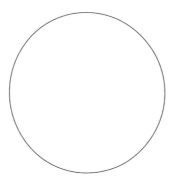

Ideas to regain balance between my work and home life:

_____

_____

To find and maintain my balance, I will:

_____

Now, record your goal in your mobile device as a calendar reminder, set to repeat weekly until you have developed new, more balanced habits.

STRATEGIES TO CONTINUE LEARNING

Striking a balance between what you know and what you need to know is also important. It can be so easy, as an experienced EI practitioner, to feel like your expertise is pretty well developed. You go to workshops and sigh, thinking *I already know this.* That's not uncommon when you have been in the field for a long time. When you are new to the EI field, you can feel like a sponge, trying to soak up so much information at once that it can be overwhelming. Maybe you are in the middle here, not a newbie but also not a 20-year veteran. Wherever you are, there is always room to grow and always something to learn. Remember how, in Chapter 1, I compared EI practice to medical and legal practices? Just as our fellow professionals in those fields must stay current, we too have to commit to seeking out ways to remain up to date with evidence-based practices in our disciplines and in the EI field. No one can do that but us. The commitment you made to read this book speaks to your commitment to learning and growth, so I don't need to add lots of strategies here. I just have two for you to consider.

Prioritize ongoing professional development. Somewhere in your work–life balance, it is really important to add your own professional development. It might mean shifting your intervention visits around one day so you can participate in a workshop, webinar, or community of practice. Or you might need to trade a few hours in the evening to study for a class or read journal articles. How you learn is up to you, but block some time to feed your brain. Add it to your schedule. Set goals, like reading one journal article a week/month, participating in one course each year, or joining a professional learning community to explore a topic of interest over several months. Start a learning group at work or host a "lunch and learn" by inviting others to join you. Hold yourself accountable for your professional development by including it on your annual performance plan at work. I'm so proud of you for the commitment you made to read this book and do this work. You may have reached the last chapter of this book, but that does not have to be the last chapter in your professional growth. Keep going.

Think beyond the single workshop. It's so easy to sign up for a webinar or attend a conference and cross professional development off the list. Here's a hard reality: Without spreading your learning experience beyond that single session, it's much less likely that you will take what you learned and integrate it into your practices. Try thinking beyond that single workshop and looking for training opportunities that have multiple components that extend your learning. Look for activities that include coaching or mentoring, video reflection, multiple training sessions, or other follow-up activities that help you use what you learned. If the training does not offer these, design them for yourself. Attend that workshop, and then commit to bringing what you learned back to your team. Hold yourself accountable for sharing what you learned with at least three other people. Find two additional resources on the training topic to access and use following the event. Host a book study with colleagues using this book you are almost finished reading. If you truly want to continue to deepen your practice, you will find that sharing what you learned with others and other ongoing efforts outside of the single workshop will make all the difference.

Pause
to PLAN

Instructions: Consider what your key takeaways are from this chapter. Think about what you still need to know or what your next steps are for continuing this journey. Jot down ideas about topics that you would like to explore and how you might do that. Again, set a goal for your professional development and post it somewhere visible as a reminder.

Key takeaway(s) from this chapter	What I still need to know
Next steps/activities	How and when I will learn more

Take a photo of this page with your mobile device. Attach the photo to an e-mail and share it with your supervisor or a colleague. Ask them to help you with your next steps or keep you on track by checking in with you once a month about your efforts toward those next steps.

YOUR JOURNEY

This chapter has really been about you. You are the person who chose to dedicate time to do the work in this book. You are also the person who will need to continue to reflect and be mindful about evolving your practices after you reach the last page. Only you can do that for yourself. Achieving a deeper understanding of EI practice is not something you can check off of a list (and believe me, if you could, I would know because I love lists). It is an ongoing process of introspection, reflection, self-assessment, learning, and development. Just as the children and families we support continue to grow and learn, so will you.

I hope this book has provided you the time and space to examine what you do on a deeper level. We have explored the idea that EI is a practice that you cultivate. We've reviewed fundamental concepts that link our work to the mission of EI so we can facilitate intervention visits that offer caregivers and children active, engaging opportunities to learn using their own interactions, activities, routines, materials, and interests. We dove deep into adult learning so you would have the foundation you need to understand how to facilitate learning in caregivers who are our best allies in intervention. We tossed around lots of ideas about how to gather the meaningful information needed to individualize your support while appreciating families for the wonderful, knowledgeable partners they are. We grounded our intervention in the intake, evaluation, assessment, and IFSP development processes, and then we reflected on what a balanced intervention visit really looks like. Hopefully, the seven steps and tons of strategies you learned in Chapter 5 for conducting balanced intervention visits will continue to guide you as you share your expertise and value what caregivers bring to each visit. I encourage you to periodically revisit the self-assessments and activities throughout this book. Over time and with practice, you may find that your answers change, and that's okay. Use these tools to reflect, check in, and keep yourself on the path. Use the self-care strategies in this last chapter to improve how you manage your work and, please, take care of your own needs.

Every day in EI is made up of tiny, wondrous moments. I hope that, in diving deep here, you have strengthened your appreciation of the power of these moments and your influence on them. I hope, every day, that you embrace the part you play in the development of a tiny, unique human being and in the empowerment and learning of a precious caregiver. When you stumble, when you fall back into old practices, when you just can't seem to figure out how to help that caregiver learn, I truly hope you will care for yourself and give yourself some grace. Take a deep breath and sit with your struggle. Acknowledge it as an inevitable part of the work you do and look for the learning opportunity in the challenge. When you knock on that door and you hear those tiny feet scatter, remind yourself that you are doing your best and that you are ready. Know that what you do, and how you do it, truly matters. I wish you all the best in your journey, my friend.

> **DO YOUR LITTLE BIT OF GOOD WHERE YOU ARE: IT'S THOSE LITTLE BITS OF GOOD PUT TOGETHER THAT OVERWHELM THE WORLD.**
>
> —Desmond Tutu

Author Answers

CHAPTER 2

Fundamentals Word Cloud (page 16)

Active participation, Adult learning, Awareness, Balanced intervention, Between visits, Build upon, Capacity building, Caregiver, Challenges, Decision making, Everyday learning opportunities, Family centered, Flexibility, Generalization, Interactions, Mission, Reflection, Relationship, Responsive, Routines

Scenario 1 (page 22)

1. Was Eli successful with implementing the mission of EI? Why or why not?

Eli started out on the right track for implementing the mission when he was responsive to Selina's concern and asked if she would like help. His intervention approach derailed when he used a passive tactic to try to help before he had enough information to know what to suggest. Eli tossed out suggestions to address the problem that were not particularly helpful because he did not have a good understanding of the problem or what Selina has already tried. When he was unable to help, he explained away the behavior as typical of children Max's age and stopped problem solving by telling Selina to wait it out. Eli seemed to resume his more child-focused approach by directing attention back to his play with Max and his focus on promoting Max's communication in a play routine. In this scenario, Eli was not successful with implementing the mission because he does not actively build on what the family is already doing, provide effective assistance to the caregiver, or explore how to promote Max's development during the naturally occurring car seat routine.

2. What could Eli have done differently to embed family-centered, capacity-building practices into the visit?

Eli needs to learn more about the routine before he can help. Some ideas for learning more include 1) asking Selina what she had already tried before giving suggestions, 2) observing the typical car seat routine to help Selina identify strategies that she could try to improve the routine, or 3) asking Selina to have her partner record the routine so they could watch the video and problem-solve at the next visit. He could also wonder with Selina about why Max might be feeling upset in the car seat, which could lead to building responsiveness to Max's cues and brainstorming about possible intervention strategies. By intentionally taking the time to learn more about the situation, Eli's suggestions would more likely be helpful and his support would be better aligned with the mission of EI.

Scenario 2 (page 23)

1. Was Eli successful with implementing the mission of EI? Why or why not?

Yes, Eli was successful because he provided support that built on what Selina had already tried to improve a problematic family routine. He also directly assisted Selina by exploring the problem and coaching her through trying intervention strategies that enhanced Max's ability to use his skills to get in and out of the car seat without becoming upset. He approached the challenge from a family-centered, capacity-building perspective to help Selina identify the learning opportunities inherent in the routine.

2. What family-centered practices did Eli use to build Selina's capacity to solve the problem?

Eli was responsive to Selina's concern and asked if she wanted help, thereby giving her the decision-making power to decide how to proceed. After learning much more about the situation, Eli was able to individualize the support he provided and help Selina identify and practice using intervention strategies that seemed to make Max feel better about being in the car seat. Eli built on what the family was already doing and assisted Selina by helping her reflect on what she knew about Max (e.g., how he climbed into the high chair). He made informed suggestions, modeled when necessary, and coached Selina as she practiced using several strategies that fit into her interaction with her son. Eli was able to combine his expertise with all that Selina knew so that they could work together to change a challenging situation into an easier routine. These improvements opened up a new learning opportunity that encouraged Max's independence, promoted his growing communication abilities, and expanded his positive social-emotional skills. Hopefully, Selina also learned how to think through the situation and problem-solve so that she will be more confident with solving similar problems in the future, meaning that her capacity to solve these problems for herself, without Eli, may have grown through this experience. This is important, because Eli will not be there to help after Max eventually leaves EI.

3. What percentage of time did Eli spend engaging the caregiver? The child?

Caregiver: _60_ %

Child: _40_ %

4. What are the main differences you see between Scenarios 1 and 2? Why do these differences matter?

In Scenario 1, Eli seems more focused on Max and the impact he (Eli) can have on Max's development during floor play. In Scenario 2, Eli is more family focused and balances his time supporting both Max and Selina. Eli's "intervention" in Scenario 1 takes much less time and is less effective than in Scenario 2, where he takes time to observe and coach Selina rather than just making general verbal suggestions. Scenario 1 involves capacity building, whereas Scenario 2 seems much more child focused, as if the parent's concern is a side note to the intervention Eli is providing to the child. Scenario 1 would likely leave the mother frustrated and feeling unsupported, whereas Scenario 2 would more likely leave her with a plan for what to do to improve the routine. She has the opportunity to practice using new strategies with her service provider's support in Scenario 2, which also builds her capacity to use those strategies between visits when she and her son try to run errands. Scenario 2 is more impactful and starts an ongoing process of support, whereas the support goes cold quickly in Scenario 1.

Pause and Reflect (page 31)

Examples of statements or open-ended questions to help the father think about what he did and interpret the impact on his son's positioning:

You did a great job with remembering the pillow supports we practiced last time.

What do you notice about Devon's body now that you've added the pillow?

If we want to help Devon sit upright here in the highchair, what do you think would help?

Pause to Practice (page 33)

	Intervention 1: Identify natural learning opportunities	Intervention 2: Strengthen parent–child relationships and responsiveness	Intervention 3: Emphasize caregiver awareness and interpretation	Intervention 4: Facilitate active participation, reflection, and decision making
Suki coaches Lexi's grandmother as they pause on the porch swing so Lexi can practice signing to get her grandmother to continue swinging.	X	X		X
Janika points out when Silas looks at a toy and helps his child care provider recognize that this is how Silas is letting her know his preference for play.		X	X	
Sarah joins Akeno and his mother at the community pool to help her identify ways for Akeno to work his muscles while they enjoy the water.	X		X	X
Alex reflects with Darcy's father about how when he offered the spoon to her left versus her right side, she seemed to find it more easily in her visual field.			X	X

Note: Any of these examples could reflect all or most of the interventions. For instance, if Alex is joining the family's breakfast routine and helping Darcy's father to read her cues during feeding (in addition to finding the best place in her visual field for her to locate the spoon), then Interventions 1 and 2 would also be implemented. If, however, Alex and Darcy's father are practicing with a spoon outside of a natural meal or snack time, then Intervention 1 would not be happening because the activity would not be occurring during a natural learning opportunity. Similarly, when Sarah joins Akeno's family at the pool, she would be implementing Intervention 2 if she were coaching his mother through moving her son in the water. If, however, Sarah is in the water with Akeno herself and his mother is watching from the poolside, the opportunity to implement Intervention 2 may be missed. Make sense?

CHAPTER 3

Pause to Think (page 46)

Components of Adult Learning Theory	Application in Early Intervention
Adult learners like to have some control over what they learn.	*Give caregivers control over what they learn by asking about their needs and priorities. Ask for their permission to share ideas or tackle a problem and respond appropriately, even if that means that you have to put aside a concern you have if the caregiver says no (such as when we are concerned about screen time but the caregiver is not). You can ask caregivers how they typically like to learn new things (e.g., by reading a handout, watching a video, using an app) and provide information they want using that method whenever possible. You can also be sure that individualized family service plan (IFSP) outcomes are based on what is important to the caregiver. Integrating what the caregiver and family need the child to be able to do into outcomes is a great way to give control and acknowledge the caregiver's lead role in encouraging the child's development.*
Adults want to learn information that is immediately relevant, solves problems, and meets needs.	*Be sure that IFSP outcomes have family priorities, concerns, and needs as their foundation. You can also explore what is immediately relevant and problematic during the intake and assessment by asking questions that relate the developmental tasks you are examining to the child's functioning in everyday life. Rather than focus on whether the child can use a tripod grasp (jargon alert), ask the caregiver about how the child picks up heerios on the highchair tray. You can also be mindful of checking in with families frequently to revisit priorities and be responsive when new challenges arise. Be flexible with the intervention supports you provide, adjusting them as needed in response to the caregiver's needs and new challenges.*
Adults need to understand how learning will occur, what they are being taught, and why it is important.	*Be intentional about asking the caregiver how he or she would like to learn to use the strategy. Provide opportunities for the caregiver to make choices about how learning will occur, such as by choosing which strategy to try, during which routine or activity the three of you will try the strategy, or perhaps the caregiver would prefer to watch you first, then try it, etc. Explain the intervention strategy you or the caregiver will use, what using it will look like, and why it is important or how it might help the caregiver and/or the child. Be specific and check for understanding. Recognize that although you may think a strategy is important or appropriate, the caregiver may not, so always explain your idea and then give the caregiver the choice of whether to try it. With time, you might not need to explain in such detail as the caregiver becomes more comfortable and knowledgeable about intervention, but always check in to support understanding and answer any questions. Check in again after the caregiver has used the strategy to see if it was useful and addressed the need or if it needs to be adjusted.*

Components of Adult Learning Theory	Application in Early Intervention
Adults bring their prior knowledge and experience to any learning situation.	*Applying this component requires that you mindfully approach intervention with a healthy respect for what the caregiver brings to the table. Check in with yourself about each family and identify the strengths you see. When working with caregivers, ask open-ended questions to help them think about what they already know, what they have already tried, and how they can use this information going forward. Help them think about why something worked or did not work by specifically asking what they think. Ask about what the caregiver did with other children to address a similar challenge. Use this information to ground the IFSP outcomes and service delivery. Before you jump in with suggestions, try to ask even just one question about prior knowledge and experience. This acknowledges what the caregiver already knows and does, and thus builds capacity, but it also provides you with valuable information on which to base individualized intervention suggestions.*

CHAPTER 4

Pause to Practice (page 76)

Yes/No or Close-Ended Questions	Open-Ended Questions
Does your child say any words yet?	*What do you hear your child say or try to say? How does your child communicate with you?*
Would you like to tell me about your day?	*How do you and your child like to spend your days? What is a typical day like for you and your child?*
Do you have any concerns?	*What concerns do you have about your child's development? What goes well during the day and what do you or your child find challenging?*
Can your baby sit up?	*What positions does your baby like to play in? How does your baby do with sitting up? What does it look like when your baby tries to sit up?*
Do you want the physical therapist to come to see you once a week?	*How often do you think it would be helpful to have the physical therapist visit? We can do visits weekly, every other week, or monthly—what sounds best to you?*

Pause to Think (page 78)

What time does Mason get up in the morning?		He loves spinning bowls on the kitchen floor and lining up his toy cars on the windowsill.
What are Mason's favorite things to do?		He takes my hand and pulls me to the kitchen when he's thirsty or hungry. It's hard to figure out what he wants and we both get frustrated sometimes. I just have to keep showing him things in the fridge until I figure it out.
Can Mason put any pieces in a puzzle yet?		8 a.m.
How does Mason let you know when he wants something to eat or drink?		I wish we could play together and he would talk like my other son. It's hard because he tantrums a lot during the day.
What would you like to be able to do with Mason?		No, should he be able to?
Does Mason eat a variety of foods?		Yes

CHAPTER 5

Pause to Practice (page 131)

"I really liked how you used a soft voice to prepare Amber for calming down. I know the tickle game is her favorite, but I think it might have excited her instead of calmed her down. What do you think? She loves being close to you so let's think of ways you can be together to help her calm herself before nap."

References

Amen, D. G. (2015). *Change your brain, change your life.* Harmony Books.

Bailey, D. B., Raspa, M., & Fox, L. C. (2012). What is the future of family outcomes and family-centered services? *Topics in Early Childhood Special Education, 31*(4), 216–223. doi:10.1177/0271121411427077

Barton, E. E., & Fettig. A. (2013). Parent-implemented interventions for young children with disabilities: A review of fidelity features. *Journal of Early Intervention, 35*(2), 194–219. doi:10.1177/1053815113504625

Bodhidharma. (1987.) The Zen teachings of Bodhidharma (Red Pine, Trans.). http://users.libero.it/seza/bodhidharma.pdf

Braceland, F. J. (April 2003). *O magazine.*

Broggi, M. B., & Sabatelli, R. (2010). Parental perceptions of the parent–therapist relationship: Effects on outcomes in early intervention. *Physical & Occupational Therapy in Pediatrics, 30*(3), 234–247. doi:10.3109/01942631003757602

Bronfenbrenner, U. (1979). *The ecology of human development.* Harvard University Press.

Bronfenbrenner, U. (1986). Ecology of the family as a context for human development: Research perspectives. *Developmental Psychology, 22*(6), 723–742.

Brown, J. A., & Woods, J. J. (2015). Effects of a triadic parent-implemented home-based communication intervention for toddlers. *Journal of Early Intervention, 37*, 1–25. doi:10.1177/1053815115589350

Bruder, M. B. (2010). Early childhood intervention: A promise to children and families for their future. *Exceptional Children, 76*(3), 339–355. Retrieved from https://journals.sagepub.com/home/ecx

Buckley, J. (2013). *Prelude to a hero.* On the Fly Publications.

Campbell, P. H., & Sawyer, L. B. (2009). Changing early intervention providers' home visiting skills through participation in professional development. *Topics in Early Childhood Special Education, 28*(4), 219–234. doi:10.1177/0271121408328481

Childress, D. C. (2015). Implementing intervention in everyday routines, activities, and settings. In S. A. Raver & D. C. Childress (Eds.), *Family-centered early intervention: Supporting infants and toddlers in natural environments* (pp. 75–106). Paul H. Brookes Publishing Co.

Childress, D. C. (2017). *Enhancing early interventionists' abilities to support caregiver learning through multi-component, technology-mediated inservice professional development.* [Doctoral dissertation, Old Dominion University]. ODU Digital Commons. Retrieved from https://digitalcommons.odu.edu/cdse_etds/2/

Church, E., Bland, P., & Church, B. (2010). Supporting quality staff development with best-practice aligned policies. *Emporia State Research Studies, 46*(2), 44–47. Retrieved from https://outlier.uchicago.edu/computerscience/OS4CS/landscapestudy/resources/Church-Bland-and-Church-2010.pdf

Covey, S. R. (2004). *The 7 habits of highly effective people: Powerful lessons in personal change.* Free Press.

Dodinsky. (2013). *In the garden of thoughts.* Sourcebooks.

Dunst, C. J. (2015). Improving the design and implementation of in-service professional development in early childhood intervention. *Infants & Young Children, 28*(3), 210–219. doi:10.1097/IYC.0000000000000042

Dunst, C. J., Bruder, M. B., & Espe-Sherwindt, M. (2014). Family capacity-building in early childhood intervention: Does context and setting matter? *School Community Journal, 24*(1), 37–48. Retrieved from http://www.adi.org/journal/2014ss/DunstBruderEspe-SherwindtSpring2014.pdf

Dunst, C. J., & Trivette, C. M. (2009). Using research evidence to inform and evaluate early childhood intervention practices. *Topics in Early Childhood Special Education, 29*(1), 40–52. doi:10.1177/0271121408329227

Dunst, C. J., Trivette, C. M., & Deal, A. G. (2011). Effects of in-service training on early intervention practitioners' use of family-systems intervention practices in the USA. *Professional Development in Education, 37*(2), 181–196. doi:10.1080/19415257.2010.527779

Dunst, C. J., Trivette, C. M., Humphries, T., Raab, M., & Roper, N. (2001). Contrasting approaches to natural learning environment interventions. *Infants & Young Children, 14*(2). Retrieved from https://journals.lww.com/iycjournal/Citation/2001/14020/Contrasting_Approaches_to_Natural_Learning.7.aspx

Early Childhood Outcomes Center. (2005). *Family and child outcomes for early intervention and early childhood special education.* Retrieved from https://ectacenter.org/~pdfs/eco/ECO _Outcomes_4-13-05.pdf

Friedman, M., Woods, J., & Salisbury, C. (2012). Caregiver coaching strategies for early intervention providers: Moving toward operational definitions. *Infants & Young Children, 25*(1), 62–82.

Goldstein, J., & Kornfield, J. (2001). *Seeking the heart of wisdom: The path to meditation.* Shambhala Publications.

Headspace.com. (2019). *What is meditation?* Retrieved from https://www.headspace.com/meditation -101/what-is-meditation

IDEA Infant Toddler Coordinators Association. (2019). *2019 Tipping points annual survey: State challenges.* Retrieved from https://www.ideainfanttoddler.org/pdf/2019-ITCA-State -Challenges-Report.pdf

Individuals with Disabilities Education Improvement Act (IDEA) of 2004, PL 108-446, 20 U.S.C. §§ 1400 *et seq.*

Joyce, B., & Showers, B. (2002). *Student achievement through staff development.* Association for Supervision and Curriculum Development.

Jung, L. (2003). More is better: Maximizing natural learning opportunities. *Young Exceptional Children, 6*(3), 21–26. doi:10.1177/109625060300600303

Kemp, P., & Turnbull, A. P. (2014). Coaching with parents in early intervention: An interdisciplinary research synthesis. *Infants & Young Children, 27*(4), 305–324. doi:10.1097/IYC.0000000000000018

Kingsford, J. (2016). UNJUGGLED: Lessons from a decade of blending business, babies, balance, and big dreams. https://www.amazon.com/UNJUGGLED-Lessons-Blending-Business-Balance-ebook /dp/B01M0PB2AI

Knowles, M. S., Holton, E. F., & Swanson, R. A. (1998). *The adult learner* (5th ed.). Gulf.

Knowles, M. S., Holton, E. F., & Swanson, R. A. (2012). *The adult learner* (7th ed.). Routledge.

Kolb, D. A. (1984). *Experiential learning: Experience as the source of learning and development.* Prentice Hall.

Kretlow, A. G., & Bartholomew, C. C. (2010). Using coaching to improve the fidelity of evidence-based practices: A review of studies. *Teacher Education and Special Education, 33*(4), 279–299. doi:10.1177/0888406410371643

Lorio, C. M., Romano, M., Woods, J. J., & Brown, J. (2020). A review of problem-solving and reflection as caregiver coaching strategies in early intervention. *Infants & Young Children, 33*(1), 35–70. doi:10.1097/IYC.0000000000000156

Mahoney, G. (2009). Relationship focused intervention (RFI): Enhancing the role of parents in children's developmental intervention. *International Journal of Early Childhood Special Education, 1*(1), 79–94. Retrieved from http://www.int-jecse.net/issues.asp?u=11

Maturana, E. R., & Woods, J. (2012). Technology-supported performance-feedback for early intervention home visiting. *Topics in Early Childhood Special Education, 32*(1), 14–23. doi:10/1177/0271121411434935

McWilliam, R. (2000). It's only natural. . .to have early intervention in environments where it's needed. In S. Sandall & M. Ostrosky (Eds.), *Natural environments and inclusion: Young exceptional children monograph series no. 2* (pp. 17–26). Division for Early Childhood.

McWilliam, R. A. (2010). *Routines-based early intervention: Supporting young children and their families.* Paul H. Brookes Publishing Co.

McWilliam, R. A. (2012). Implementing and preparing for home visits. *Topics in Early Childhood Special Education, 31*(4), 224–231. doi:10.1177/0271121411426488

Moore, H. W., Barton, E. E., & Chironis, M. (2014). A program for improving toddler communication through parent coaching. *Topics in Early Childhood Special Education, 33*(4), 212–224. doi:10.1177/0271121413497520

National Research Council. (2000). *How people learn: Brain, mind, experience, and school.* National Academies Press.

Oprah.com. (2011, October 20). Jill Bolte Taylor's Stroke of Insight. [Video]. OWN. http://www.oprah .com/oprahs-lifeclass/jill-bolte-taylors-stroke-of-insight-video

Odom, S. L., & Wolery, M. (2003). A unified theory of practice in early intervention/early childhood special education. *Journal of Special Education, 37*(3), 164–173. doi:10.1177/00224669030370030601

Penuel, W. R., Fishman, B. J., Yamaguchi, R., & Gallagher, L. P. (2007). What makes professional development effective? Strategies that foster curriculum implementation. *American Education Research Journal, 44*(4), 921–958. doi:10.3102/0002831207308221

Raab, M., Dunst, C. J., & Trivette, C. M. (2010). Adult learning process for promoting caregiver adoption of everyday child language learning practices: Revised and updated. *Practically Speaking, 2*(1), 1–8. Retrieved from http://www.puckett.org/CECLL/ECLLReport_3_AdultLearning.pdf

Rohn, J. (2015). *Rohn: 4 straightforward steps to success.* Retrieved from https://www.success.com /rohn-4-straightforward-steps-to-success/

Rush, D. D., & Shelden, M. L. (2011). *The early childhood coaching handbook.* Paul H. Brookes Publishing Co.

Rush, D. D., & Shelden, M. L. (2020). *The early childhood coaching handbook* (2nd ed.). Paul H. Brookes Publishing Co.

Salisbury, C., Cambray-Engstrom, E., & Woods, J. (2012). Providers' reported and actual use of coaching strategies in natural environments. *Topics in Early Childhood Special Education, 32*(2), 88–98. doi:10.1177/0271121410392802

Salisbury, C. L., & Cushing, L. S. (2013). Comparison of triadic and provider-led intervention practices in early intervention home visits. *Infant & Young Children, 26*(1), 28–41. doi:10.1097/IYC.ob013e3182736fc0

Salisbury, C. L., Woods, J., & Copeland, C. (2010). Provider perspectives on adopting and using collaborative consultation in natural environments. *Topics in Early Childhood Special Education, 30*(3), 132–147. doi:10.1177/0271121409349769

Sawyer, B. E., & Campbell, P. H. (2012). Early interventionists' perspectives on teaching caregivers. *Journal of Early Intervention, 34*(2), 104–124. doi:10/1177/1053815112455363

Shellenberg, S., Negishi, M., & Eggen, P. (2011). The effects of metacognition and concrete encoding strategies on the depth of understanding in educational psychology. *Teaching Educational Psychology, 7*(2), 17–24. Retrieved from https://sites.google.com/site/teachedpsych/2011-volume-7

Sher, B. "You don't need endless time and perfect conditions." Retrieved from AZ Quotes. https://www.azquotes.com/quote/669055

Snyder, P., Hemmeter, M. L., & McLaughlin, T. (2011). Professional development in early childhood intervention: Where we stand on the silver anniversary of PL 94-142. *Journal of Early Intervention, 33*(4), 357–370. doi:10.1177/1053815111428336

Swanson, J., Raab, M., & Dunst, C. J. (2011). Strengthening family capacity to provide young children everyday natural learning opportunities. *Journal of Early Childhood Research, 9*(1), 66–80. doi:10.1177/1476718X10368588

Tomlin, A. M., & Viehweg, S. A. (2016). *Tackling the tough stuff: A home visitor's guide to supporting families at risk.* Paul H. Brookes Publishing Co.

Trivette, C. M., Dunst, C. J., & Hamby, D. W. (2010). Influences of family-systems intervention practices on parent–child interactions and child development. *Topics in Early Childhood Special Education, 30*(1), 3–19. doi:10.1177/0271121410364250

Trivette, C. M., Dunst, C. J., Hamby, D. W., & O'Herin, C. E. (2009). *Characteristics and consequences of adult learning methods and strategies.* Research Brief Volume 3, Number 1. Tots n Tech Research Institute. Retrieved from https://www.buildinitiative.org/portals/0/uploads/documents/resource-center/diversity-and-equity-toolkit/adultlearning_rev7-04-09.pdf

Tutu. D. (2015, October 7). 10 pieces of wisdom from Desmond Tutu on his birthday.

van Kersteren, M. T. R., Rijpkema, M., Ruiter, D. J., Morris, R. G. M., & Fernandez, G. (2014). Building on prior knowledge: Schema-dependent encoding processes relate to academic performance. *Journal of Cognitive Neuroscience, 26*(10), 2250–2261. doi:10.1162/jocn_a_00630

VEIPD Videos. (2015, July 31). *The goal of early intervention: Roman's mother.* YouTube. Retrieved from https://youtu.be/LicqxtLsk_k

Warren, R. (2013). *The purpose driven life: What on Earth am I here for?* Zondervan.

Woods, J. (2019). *Family guided routines based intervention: Key indicators manual.* Retrieved from http://fgrbi.fsu.edu/handouts/approach5/KIManual2019.pdf

Woods, J. J., & Brown, J. A. (2011). Integrating family capacity-building and child outcomes to support social communication development in young children with autism spectrum disorder. *Topics in Language Disorders, 31*(3), 235–246. doi:10.1097/TLD.ob013e318227fde4

Woods, J. J., & Lindeman, D. P. (2008). Giving and gathering information with families. *Infants & Young Children, 21*(4). doi:10.1097/01.IYC.0000336540.60250.f2

Woods, J. J., Wilcox, M. J., Friedman, M., & Murch, T. (2011). Collaborative consultation in natural environments: Strategies to enhance family-centered supports and services. *Language, Speech, and Hearing Services in Schools, 42*, 379–392. doi:10.1044/0161-1461(2011/10-0016)

Workgroup on Principles and Practices in Natural Environments, OSEP TA Community of Practice: Part C Settings. (2008, March). *Agreed upon mission and key principles for providing early intervention services in natural environments.* Retrieved from http://ectacenter.org/~pdfs/topics/families/Finalmissionandprinciples3_11_08.pdf

Yang, C-H., Houssain, S. Z., & Sitharthan, G. (2013). Collaborative practices in early childhood intervention from the perspective of the service providers. *Infants & Young Children, 26*(1), 57–73. doi:10/1097/IYC.ob013e3182736cbf

Index

Page numbers followed by *f* indicate figures.

Parent-implemented interventions, 42
Parenting, learning new skills in, 26
Passive observation
    and adult learning, 9–10, 31, 122
    during modeling, 122
Physical barriers, being mindful about, 72–73
PL 108-446, 5, 75, 98*f*, 104
Planning
    and adult learning, 47–48
    joint, 81, 110, 111, 114, 133–134
    for between visits, 132–134
Positioning
    mindful, 44–45, 72–73
    tips for, 114
Practice
    celebrating, 128
    facilitating, 120–129
    fading support during, 127
    and learning, 30, 47, 48, 56–57
    modeling followed by, 121, 122
    in real contexts and in real time, 124–125
    reflection and feedback on, 129–132
Prior knowledge
    in adult learning, 46–48, 50–51, 69, 77, 130
    gathering information about, 69
Priorities
    vs. concerns, 68
    discussion about, 115
    example of, 69
    gathering information about, 67–69, 88*f*
    identifying, 48
    integrating into IFSP outcomes, 48, 95*f*, 96*f*
Privacy, 75
Problem solving
    feedback and, 58
    flexibility and, 49
    during intervention visits, 118–120
    strategies for, 118–119
Professional development, 2–3, 8, 157–158

Quality assurance (QA), 151
Questions
    about priorities, 115
    context of, 87*f*
    for decision making, 133
    for facilitating caregiver practice, 121
    for feedback, 130–131, 133
    friendly, 84, 87*f*, 114
    for information gathering, 68, 69, 70
    inviting caregivers to ask, 89*f*
    for modeling, 122
    for observation, 116
    preparing caregivers for, 74–75
    reflective, 130–131
    yes/no (close-ended), 77, 87*f*
    see also Open-ended questions

Rapport building
    body positioning and, 72–73
    dedicating time to, 71–72
    explanations and, 74–75
    problem solving and, 49
    respect and, 73, 74
    sharing personal information and, 72

trust and, 73, 74
    during visits, 71, 83–84
Reciprocal feedback, 48, 58, 129, 131
Reciprocal relationship, 66, 71–74, 77, 81, 84, 119
Record audit, 151–152
Reflection
    and adult learning, 3, 32, 47, 48, 57–60
    benefits of, 4, 32
    by caregivers, 32
    continuous, 11
    in conversation, 58
    on early intervention triad, 45
    importance of, 32
    improving, 4
    during intervention visits, 129–132
    open-ended questions and, 58
    in problem solving, 119
    sharing, 4
    strategies for, 130–131
Reflective conversation
    example of, 24
    gathering information via, 76–80
    during intervention visits, 116, 130
    purpose of, 130
Reflective journal, 11, 12, 36, 62, 100, 140
Reflective questions, 130–131
Reliability, 73
Reminders
    for early intervention providers, 151
    for intervention visits, 111, 134
Repetition, and learning, 25
Respect
    in balanced intervention, 61, 116
    being on time and, 147
    for cultural values, 20
    in rapport building, 73, 74
Responsiveness, 73, 116
Routines-based intervention, 24–27, 32, 46, 53, 61

Sandwich strategy, for feedback, 131
Scheduling intervention visits, 134–136, 146–147
Self-assessment
    about balanced intervention strategies, 106–109
    about IFSP development, 91*f*–93*f*
    about information gathering, 85–87
    about self-care, 144–146
Self-awareness
    and adult learning, 3, 32, 47, 48, 57–60
    making time for, 11
Self-care, 143–159
    challenges of, 143
    documentation strategies, 150–152
    importance of, 146
    professional development, 2–3, 8, 157–158
    self-assessment about, 144–146
    stress management, 153–157
    time management, 146–150
Self-direction, in adult learning, 46, 48
Self-reflection, 130
Service coordinators
    documentation by, 151, 152
    intake visits conducted by, 71, 83
    mindful about physical barriers and positioning, 72
    perspective of discovery of, 76